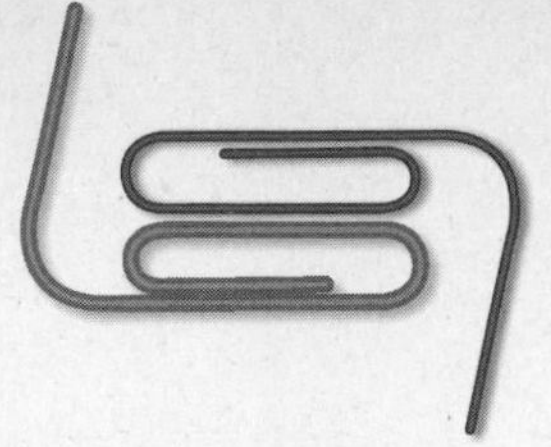

# THE KAMA SUTRA OF BUSINESS

## MANAGEMENT PRINCIPLES FROM INDIAN CLASSICS

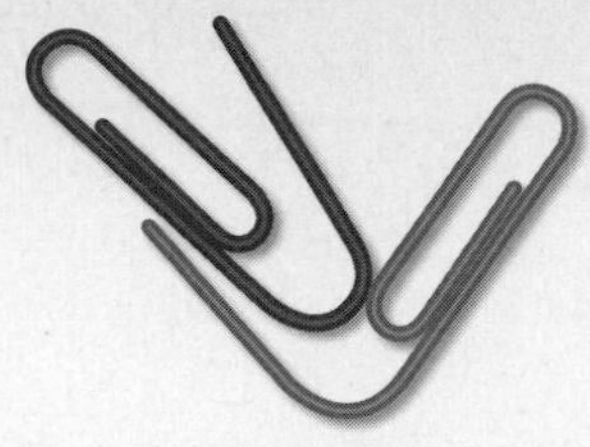

# THE KAMA SUTRA OF BUSINESS

## MANAGEMENT PRINCIPLES FROM INDIAN CLASSICS

NURY VITTACHI



BICENTENNIAL 1807 WILEY 2007 BICENTENNIAL

JOHN WILEY & SONS (ASIA) PTE LTD

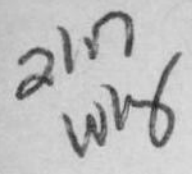




Published in 2007 by John Wiley & Sons (Asia) Pte Ltd
2 Clementi Loop, #02-01, Singapore 129809



*Other Wiley Editorial Offices*

John Wiley & Sons, 111 River Street, Hoboken, NJ 07030, USA
John Wiley & Sons, The Atrium Southern Gate, Chichester P019 8SQ, England
John Wiley & Sons (Canada) Ltd, 5353 Dundas Street West, Suite 400,
Toronto Ontario M9B 6HB. Canada
John Wiley & Sons Australia Ltd. 42 McDougall Street, Milton, Queensland 4064,
Australia
Wiley-VCH, Bosch Strasse 12, D-69469 Weinheim, Germany

*Library of Congress Cataloging-in-Publication Data*

ISBN-13-978-0-470-82223-4
ISBN-10-0-470-82223-6

Wiley Bicentennial Logo: Richard J. Pacifico
Typeset in 12/15 Points Palatino by JC Ruxpin Pte Ltd
Printed in Singapore by Saik Wah Press Pte Ltd
10 9 8 7 6 5 4 3 2 1

# TABLE OF CONTENTS

# ACKNOWLEDGMENTS

When giving talks around the world, I often ask audiences to name the huge Asian country which is set to become a dominant global economic force powered by the world's largest population.

Hands shoot up and the answer given is always China.

But the correct answer, actually, is India.

China is set firmly on the road to having the world's second biggest population; not the largest. That particular "Number One Ranking" is on its way from China to India, where it is due to arrive in less than two decades and settle for the foreseeable future.

And the numbers don't include India's immediate neighbor Pakistan, which is expected to become the fourth most populous country on the planet by 2050. Or put it this way: by 2050, India and Pakistan together will contain a significant chunk of the world's people; more individuals (1.95 billion) than all the African countries put together (1.9 billion), according to the United Nations Population Division.

India and its neighbors are going to be significant players on the world stage and yet little is known about their amazing intellectual heritage.

The original idea for this book came from C. J. Hwu, my publisher at John Wiley, and I am happy to acknowledge my debt to her for her inspiration and vision. I would also like to thank my editor, Salil Tripathi and the project coordinator Joel Balbin.

But most of all, I salute the wonderful people of India and its neighbors, for generating the wisdom that is hereby celebrated.

Nury Vittachi
Hong Kong
December 2006

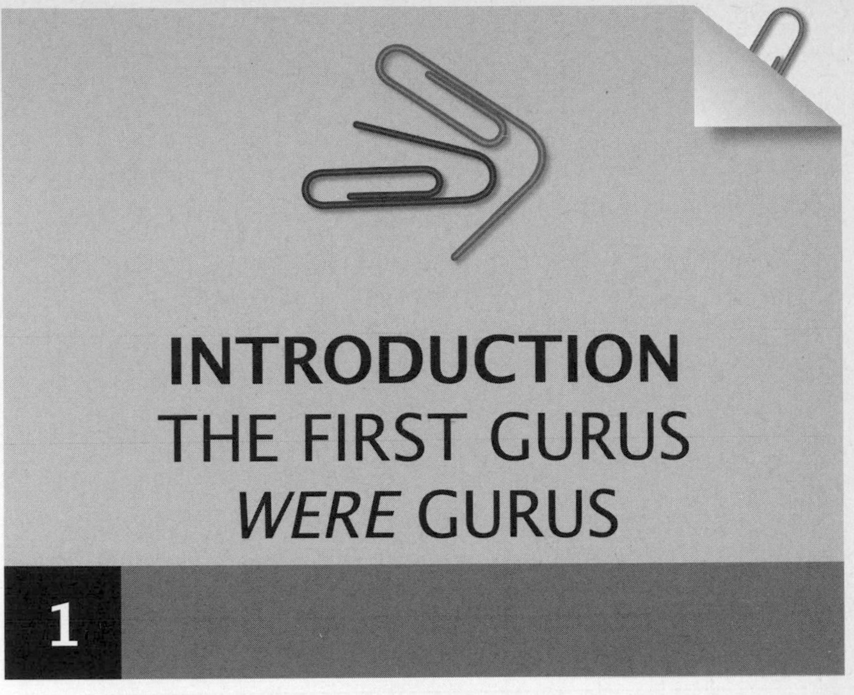

# INTRODUCTION THE FIRST GURUS *WERE* GURUS

1

## IN WHICH WE PREPARE TO UNLOCK STORES OF WISDOM FROM THE PAST

## LOST SECRETS FROM ANCIENT INDIA HAVE TRANSFORMATIVE POWER

INDIA HAS ALWAYS BEEN the source of life-transforming wisdom. From all over the world, people make pilgrimages to India to find their center, to journey inwards and to reignite their spirits. It's true today and it's been true since the dawn of recorded history.

The secrets of that rich, spiritual power are in the country's most ancient texts, the essence of which this book makes available in an appealing, fun-to-read style. And what we discover is that these classic writings aren't just for hippies. They contain remarkable practical techniques ambitious people can use to grab and retain power and; to make strategic maneuvers for success in business and politics. They also offer valuable advice on interpersonal skills and provide timeless wisdom on achieving balance in one's life.

Our title may have some readers thinking this book contains "64 positions in which you can screw your business rivals, complete with diagrams." What it really contains is far more interesting than that. It promises to enhance your performance in your professional and personal lives in countless ways, by giving you an elixir distilled from the oldest sources of all. Whether that's better than sex is for you to decide! But yes, you *will* leave your business rivals face down in the dust. Consider the following:

- The world's first management guru was a sage who used his techniques to build an empire bigger than Western Europe.
- Traders in ancient India built an Atlantis-like lost world complete with high technology, traffic jams and stone "credit cards."
- Many remarkable strategic tools for modern business leaders are hidden in humanity's oldest books, such as the *Bhagavad Gita*.
- Copies of the *Kama Sutra* in circulation in the West contain only 20% of the original text.

## THE KAMA SUTRA OF BUSINESS

THE MAN WHO WROTE the *Kama Sutra* was celibate. The ancient Indian classic, widely perceived as the world's first sex manual, is believed to have been written by a religious student who didn't even have a girlfriend.

His name was Vatsyayana, and his job was not to study sex, but God. The center of his life was his divinity studies. Yet he believed that the different aspects of life, including spirituality, materialism and sexuality, needed to be balanced. And he felt that the third of these was badly served by the existing literature. So he set himself the job of setting the record straight.

The dissertation he wrote has become famous around the globe as the ultimate book about sex. While volumes like *The Joy of Sex* have been known for decades, Vatsyayana's book has been celebrated for more than one and half millennia. It has simultaneously become one of the most banned books ever written and one of the most popular. People have feared it for more than a millennium: until recently, it was not to be found in most libraries, and even encyclopedias omitted mention of it. Yet it has been celebrated for centuries, far longer than almost any other non-religious book. Today, it is widely known around the world in multiple languages. And there are nearly two million references to it on the Internet.

The *Kama Sutra* is an enigma. It is arguably the most famous book in the world that is almost completely unknown. In other words, while almost everyone has heard of it, very few people have actually read it. And stranger still, even most of the people who think they have read it, haven't. In this sense, Vatsyayana's book could well deserve the title of "one of the most misunderstood books ever written" (along with most writings classified as holy scriptures). Today, many people still see the *Kama Sutra* as a scandalous work about things not discussed by decent folk in polite company when women and children are around. Those who are more permissive see it as a useful, adults-only catalogue of sex positions, an early equivalent of *The Joy of Sex*. And even today, computers fitted with child-protection filters will not allow web-surfers to visit many websites that mention the words "kama sutra," and probably wisely. Even people who create websites based on it invariably reveal they have misunderstood it.

The book you have in your hand presents a different view of this and other classics of ancient Indian literature. It argues that there is an enormous amount of extremely valuable information in the ancient writings of India, most of which is entirely untapped by modern, middle-class India, let alone the wider world. It takes the view that much of the wisdom of the sages and early leaders of India is not just relevant today, but provides a more useful and balanced set of guidelines for modern life than more recent equivalents. It suggests that a perspective that encompasses Eastern and Western thought is a better model for operating in today's world than the Western-dominated literature of "guides to success" in business and personal life. After all, more than half the world's population lives in Asia.

We've taken our title from the *Kama Sutra* because it is known by everyone and known by no one. In that sense, it stands for much of India's collected wisdom. Yes, that book (but not this book, sorry) includes advice on positions for copulation. Yet such material only makes up some 20% of its text. The other 80% deals with a host of other matters about life and interpersonal relationships. It also discusses wealth generation and education. It discusses ethics, rights and duties. But most of all, it focuses on creating balance in our lives. The word "kama" in the title is an ancient Sanskrit word referring to sensual pleasure. *Kama* does not lead to happiness unless it is correctly balanced with *dharma* and *artha*, says Vatsyayana, the author of the *Kama Sutra*. What does he mean by that? We'll find out in the pages that follow. I hope it'll be an interesting and enjoyable journey.

Another reason for naming this book after the *Kama Sutra* is that Vatsyayana's work is relevant, timeless, appealing, fun to read and delightfully unexpected: qualities that also apply to the stories and writings featured in this book.

## THE TOOLS TO SUCCEED

IF THERE IS ONE thing that has become abundantly clear about achievement in this technological age, it is this: the most advanced, complex and fertile piece of electrically-powered equipment in the world is neither software nor hardware—it is a piece of wetware called the human brain. In other words, each of us already has the key piece of equipment we need to change the world.

To make a great breakthrough, the only *extra* things we need are time, space and a sharp pencil. There are many people who have put together these few items and achieved great things. Let's take, for example, two celebrated modern thinkers: Albert Einstein and Stephen Hawking. Thanks to them, humanity has come to terms with amazing ideas, such as the concept that before the universe exploded into being, space was filled with nothing; not even space. It is a paradoxical notion that the two 20$^{th}$ century master scientists explain with lengthy arguments ranging from physics to philosophy.

Yet when we look back at the very oldest piece of writing in India, we find the following:

> *At the time of the beginning, there was no such thing as being; but there was also no such thing as not being.*

The unnamed writer of one of the oldest works of literary art in existence is saying that before the dawn of time, space was filled with nothing: not even emptiness. In other words, the author of the *Rig Veda*, composed more than three and a half millennia ago, had the same idea as scientists have today. This early anticipation of modern thought leads us along an intriguing avenue: *perhaps human beings really are no smarter today than they were four or five millennia ago,* at the dawn of recorded history.

We think of 5,000 years as a long time, but when we look at the whole history of humanity, it becomes merely the blink of an eye. Ancient hominids, people who walked on two legs and were part of the genus classified as *homo* have been around for more than a million years. Even if we narrow our focus down to advanced hominids with a high degree of intelligence, we find that tool-making and other skills have been with *homo sapiens* and their distant cousins and ancestors—*homo erectus, homo robustus, homo floresiensis, homo neandertalis* and others—for more than a hundred thousand years.

And yet *homo sapiens'* move from being just another creature of the forest to being a world-dominating, technology-using, miracle-maker, has happened at extremely high speed. The advanced level of self-consciousness, the intelligence and the communicative abilities that have taken us on this recent breathless journey to the age of technological miracles is not something that happened in Albert Einstein's office a few decades ago, but a change that must have taken place several thousand years ago. We gained the ability to understand ourselves, our world, our relationships, our motivations and the shapes of our lives. And the big questions of life have been considered and discussed and pontificated on by the wisest men and women continuously from that day till now. Today, we may know more facts. But that doesn't mean that we are wiser.

We can take this line of inquiry further, to notions such as this: perhaps the answers to many of the great questions that perplex humanity are not to be found through technology and the amassing of ever-bulkier collections of information, as is our wont, but can better be uncovered by other means—for example, by taking journeys through the huge, under-explored, labyrinthine space known as the human mind. As I say, the possession of facts doesn't mean that we are wiser—and may mean the opposite. Perhaps humanity's most successful thinkers are likely to be those who are *not* distracted by the so-called information tools that surround us today: the Internet and the television and electronic searchable library databases. It may well be true that the more of these information-thrusting "productivity aids" we have, the less we actually achieve in terms of measured, sustained, creative thought.

What we have done is exchanged intelligent thought for large numbers of facts. We amass libraries of books, most of which remain unread. Then the computer age comes along, and we amass an ever larger number of databases. We have more and more facts at our fingertips. But we actually *know* less and less. And with all the distractions, we spend less time thinking deeply. Our children are going to have it worse, as we fill up their timetables with extra-curricular activities and load their bedrooms and classrooms with computers and electronic toys. Of course, we do this to make them smarter, not realizing that we are doing the opposite.

Information anxiety is now a recognized psychological condition, and some people are beginning to realize that need to stop building databases and start thinking about what we already know. That's where journeys into the past become vital. We think of human society in times gone by as simpler, and more primitive. Certainly, people would have suffered less from information overload in the past. But any examination of the lives of people in history shows that interpersonal relations, office politics and financial maneuvering were as complex as ever. And while life may have been simpler, it was also starker: death was never far away, and the volatility of inter-tribal rivalries meant that human beings always had to be on their toes. The 17th century English philosopher Thomas Hobbes called life in nature to be "solitary, poor, nasty, brutish and short." Lengthy periods of peace and plenty were hard to find. You had to keep your mind sharp to survive.

The idea that ancient thinkers and classic thinking methods have much to teach us is not new. A number of classic writings have been "mined" for information that is considered valuable today. From China, Sun Tzu's *Art of War* has found new life as a classic for business strategists, and appears in the "management books" section at every airport. From Europe, we have Niccolo Machiavelli's *The Prince*, now seen as a textbook for negotiators. There has been a succession of business books that draw management lessons from people ranging from Alexander the Great to Attila the Hun. These historical leaders from Europe and North Asia have certainly provided remarkable lessons for humanity.

But many of the world's oldest recorded classics of wisdom come from middle and South Asia. These writings have been celebrated and used by people in India and its neighbors for not just hundreds of years, but millennia. Indeed, some scholars believe one of the oldest pieces of writing in existence—a series of undeciphered symbols on a rock 5,500 years old—is from the region of the Indus Valley, now located in Pakistan. This wealth of material includes stories, legends and records of people and deeds that are often startling, original and deeply thought-provoking.

Yet the remarkable wisdom they encompass has not hitherto been available in an accessible form for the modern, busy, harried, English-speaking reader. This volume humbly offers itself as an attempt to start filling that gap.

## THE FIRST GURUS

WE TALK A LOT these days about *gurus*. That term for a spiritual leader is now a common noun. A successful financier is an investment guru; an expert on setting up websites is a web guru;

a designer who can predict what people will be wearing next season is a fashion guru, and so on. Modern, technology-obsessed people are particularly fond of the word, and dictionaries of computing terms often define it by using another metaphorical noun: a *guru* is a *wizard*, they explain.

But the English word *guru* is lifted from Hindi and many other widely spoken Indian languages. These languages in turn lifted it from a Sanskrit word pronounced the same way, a very ancient term coming from Indo-European roots where we find many of the oldest words in human history. Words like these probably come from the very dawn of language, the original post-grunt system of words that linguists call proto-Indo-European, the hypothetical common ancestor of many modern languages. But for a word with such a long history, it is interesting to note that the meaning has not changed very much: it still refers to an influential leader, an expert guide. Examination of how the word is used reveals that it almost always refers to someone in the position of being a mentor, and is usually associated with something that can be defined as a movement or a uniting concept. In that sense, the modern word has maintained a link with its origins in which most gurus were spiritual teachers or pastoral leaders. It still echoes the *guru-shishya parampara,* or master-pupil, tradition of ancient India, in which pupils moved in to the master's home and performed tasks in return for knowledge. All this is obvious enough or at least easily deducible in a world where "business guru" books telling us how to make more money faster or live happier lives appear regularly on the bestseller lists. What is less obvious is this interesting fact: *the first gurus of success in business and personal development were actual gurus.*

Move over, Sun Tzu and Niccolo Machiavelli: these fabled individuals will meet their match once the writings of Chanakya, a sage in India who was born circa 350 BCE, become better known. Like those two other theorists of economic and social structures,

Chanakya was a powerful thinker, a sage, and a friend of kings and princes who wrote a book about society and governance. But while Machiavelli has become the archetype of the stop-at-nothing political plotter, we find that Chanakya's strategies are far more tricky, manipulative and cunning. He was a hot-tempered schemer with a devious turn of mind, and came up with extraordinary plans to get his own way. His list of schemes to get rid of his enemies was staggeringly long, and often included details of ways to "accidentally" drop large rocks on their heads. Picture a man who blends the cunning of Shakespeare's Iago with the practical wickedness of Wile E. Coyote from the *Roadrunner* cartoon. It sounds like an extraordinary mix, but he was highly successful, becoming the power behind the throne of one of the world's biggest empires. Indeed, social historian Professor Roger Boesche of Stanford University wrote that Machiavelli "would have been easily outmatched" by army generals reading Chanakya's works.

Chanakya can legitimately be counted as one of the world's first great business and social strategists. He discussed methods of getting power in ways that are clearly recognizable to modern analysts of the politics of business (although we no longer drop rocks on our rivals' heads, unless we are *very* desperate). He also spent a great deal of time studying social structure, and much of his writing can be seen as the work of a pioneering management guru. He wrote about leadership qualities, human resources, the importance of competition, time management and a dozen other subjects that are clearly recognizable as key themes for modern executives. But he is just one example out of many in this book.

A thinker who was arguably even more revolutionary was the unnamed man who led the building of the cities of the mysterious Meluhhan civilization and solved technological problems of architecture, engineering and water distribution that still fox people living in that area today, some 4,300 years later.

It's an incredible tale of a leader whose innovation tapped into the energy of urbanization long before the rest of humanity caught up. Those planned cities were probably the first to appear in the history of the world. And still more curiously, as recently as 100 years ago, the world knew nothing about them. Even today, new discoveries are regularly being made about the Meluhhans and their land.

But then again, perhaps the most astonishing story of all is that of Ashoka, who more than two millennia ago built a community that anticipated huge numbers of things we think of as belonging to post-industrial society. He built a health care system, funding it with taxpayers' money, to raise the general fitness level of his populace. He was a passionate "greenie," caring for forests and starting an environmental fund. And he even created an animal welfare movement. But before doing any of that, he had also killed an unimaginably large number of people: he was a complex man, as we shall see.

There are other tidbits I could throw in here to tease you to read the rest of the book, but why waste time? This volume is brief enough, and you will quickly meet some amazing individuals and learn from their lives and their writings.

But let's play devil's advocate for a moment. We're talking about India. Can ideas from that country serve as an example for people today? People outside that nation may well be skeptical. They usually think of the huge south Asian country as a poor, sprawling, ill-managed place struggling to feed its out-of-control population, even if it does score some good figures on the economic development growth chart these days. What does India have to teach the world?

This is not an unnatural reaction, although it can be set right quickly enough. Yes, India has been through some difficult struggles, particularly in the past century, but it is important to remember that for much of recorded history, India was a major and dominant force in international trade, with a succession of wealthy and military empires. In the ancient past, it was an innovative society responsible for many world "firsts." Indeed, the Meluhhan civilization is arguably the greatest of all the early human conurbations in terms of size and development. India is the place where humans first learned to write. The first wheeled transport came from India, as did the first spinning of cotton on a mass scale. India is the place where some of the fundamental tools of mathematics were developed, making computer science possible. India's emperors and their sages developed methods of governance that are models for today's societies.

But little is known about Indian history outside the country itself—which is a great shame, since these histories are filled with breathtaking examples of human achievement. To give just one example, take the Indian city of Vijayanagar, which thrived between the 14th and 16th centuries in the south of the country. At its height of influence, it was a huge empire that stretched across the country. The flourishing main city was 100 kilometers in circumference, and its trading partners stretched from Europe to East Asia. It was known for its writers and artists. When its army was finally defeated at a battle in 1565, the sole ruling survivor left Vijayanagar with his treasure—carried on the backs of 550 elephants. Now that's what any modern executive would count as a decent-sized golden parachute.

## CONNECTING WITH A SOURCE OF TREASURE

IN THIS VOLUME, WE will take you on a journey through the remarkable writings of ancient India; historical commentaries, tales, myths and legends that contain the distilled wisdom of several millennia of human thought. We'll also meet the people who composed the writings (such as Vatsyayana), who featured in the works (such as Siddhartha) or who lived by the ancient texts (such as Chandragupta).

The man who wrote the *Arthashastra* comes across very much as an inveterate note-taker in the classic sense, always jotting down ideas and schemes and aphorisms. We will also deal with one of the great empire-builders of world history: a man named Chandragupta Maurya, who was not a writer, but who lived according to many of the rules in the *Arthashastra*. And then there was Siddhartha Gautama, who did not write a book himself, but whose followers recorded his life wisdom, and who became founder of one of the world's leading faiths. That tale links up with the story of the Emperor Ashoka, who was a sort of "rock diarist." In a very rational bid for immortality (for his philosophy, not for himself) he wrote his thoughts on massive slabs of stone which were erected around his country and in neighboring lands.

Many of the stories circulating in India about the people featured in this book are clearly fairytales written by highly inventive people: Siddhartha Gautama, for example, is said to be a god-man with blue eyes and blue *eyebrows*; Ashoka is said to have killed 99 half-brothers; Arjuna's chariot driver is said to have been a god with superpowers worthy of Superman. But this book is intended for modern working people, and so we have done our best to be rational, intelligent and to review the lives of famous people with a healthy dose of skepticism. We are focusing only on human beings who really lived, and are taking inspiration from real achievements, not fantasies. In other words, we've searched for historicity and authenticity, and skipped almost all of the obviously invented ones.

At the same time, there are some irresistible narratives in ancient Indian history, some of which are likely to be more or less rooted in fact. These I have included, and left them in their popular, narrative form: they are easier to read and to remember that way. Some strict, professional historians (I am not one) might be horrified at this, but a little leeway can be very valuable. A small degree of imaginative reconstruction has been allowed for the sake of making the narratives vivid and readable. While there were obviously no voice recorders in those days, some of the old writings succeed remarkably well in capturing the personalities of their authors.

As for the direct quotes from the ancient texts, I have moved away from the original English translations, which are often archaic, and have put them into clear, plain, modern English. While a fairly generous amount of material from these classic works is quoted, directly and indirectly, you will not find the full texts in this book. This volume, I hope, will inspire you to identify the classic writings that most appeal to you, and go and find the original texts.

But let me first introduce your tour guide. The present writer is an author of fiction and non-fiction books who spends a great deal of his time speaking at corporate conferences. As such, he is very familiar with the category of books and speeches sometimes known as "business inspiration." Such material is inevitably filled with quotes from Western business leaders. Some of it is fine, but much of it is not nearly as thought-provoking and original as the management and leadership inspiration we get from the East. The old Indian sages were smart, they whisked spiritual and business and personal advice together until it became a luscious frothy mixture, and added a generous sprinkle of Zen-like Buddhism on top.

And although the material is old, it comes across as fresh. We start and end this book with references to the *Kama Sutra*, but there are other wonderful texts featured here, such as the *Bhagavad Gita,* which tells the gripping tale of a prince who hesitates on the battlefield shortly before a war because the people he has to kill are his estranged cousins, and if he does not, he will be killed by them. Like the *Kama Sutra*, this is a book the title of which many people will be familiar with. But the actual story, the history behind it, and the lessons we learn from it, will be fresh to the vast majority of readers. And there are many quotations from the works of Chanakya, which are unknown outside India and, sadly, largely uncelebrated even within the community that produced them. It is a privilege for the present author to be able to represent them to both India and to the world at large.

It is likely that this work also contains references to books and people that you have never heard of—but once they become familiar, I suspect you'll find it hard to forget them. We are about to embark on a journey during which we will meet people and read books through which we can truly revitalize our lives in business and at home: it should be an interesting and refreshing experience.

The world may well be a very different place now in comparison to what it was like 40 centuries ago. But human beings? There probably isn't an iota of difference. The bio-electrical piece of wetware that powers society has never needed to be upgraded.

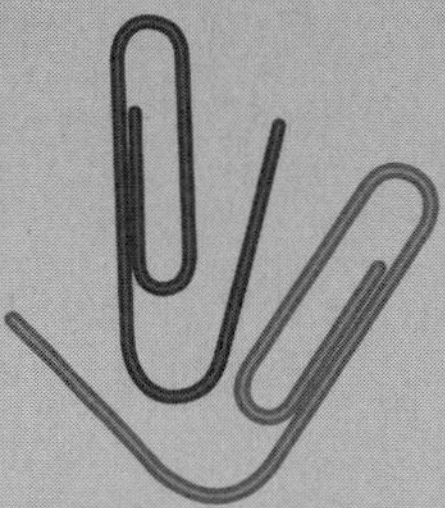

# THE WORLD'S FIRST MANAGEMENT CONSULTANT

2

**A SAGE ASSEMBLING MATERIAL FOR THE *ARTHASHASTRA*, THE FIRST BUSINESS BOOK EVER WRITTEN, DEFINES STRATEGIC PRINCIPLES THAT STILL CONTAIN TRANSFORMATIVE POWER.**

## DEAD MAN WALKING

A DEAD MAN WALKED into the village and drifted toward the tree at the center of it. His legs were moving and he appeared to be breathing, but his eyes were glassy and unmoving, his face an expressionless mask.

He cut a curious figure. No one would have considered him handsome, with his pinched features, dark skin, thin body and missing teeth, but he nevertheless gave the impression of rank: he was a well-dressed man, in expensive robes—clearly a nobleman, or an official, or a high-ranking monk. There was one incongruity: while his clothes indicated good grooming, his hair was shaved at the front and long and loose at the back, hanging down behind him. It seemed to be missing a hair band. He was probably carrying pieces of parchment, being an obsessive reader and writer. But the most notable thing about him would have been the expression on his face: a look of such utter lifelessness that he looked like an ambulant corpse.

Vishnugupta Chanakya's head was numb. A proud and arrogant man, he had lived a charmed life until now—and on this single day it had all come crashing down. His rise to greatness had started in his infancy, and his meteoric climb had barely paused for a day. He had excelled at school, joined the finest university in the region at the age of 16, and then become a teacher/guru there. In recent months, the growth of his power base had been particularly swift and exhilarating, as he had moved from academia to being a member of the ruling classes. He was seen as one of the most intelligent and capable men in the land, and deserving of his place among the ruler's special advisors. It seemed as if he could do no wrong.

And yet on this grim day his career had hit a stone wall. Chanakya was a royal court official, in charge of the *Sungha*, the royal welfare trust. But his carefully constructed relationship with the ruler, King Dhana of the Nanda Dynasty, had deteriorated sharply, and eventually imploded. It had never been an easy ride: their working relationship had started off awkwardly with the brutal ruler apparently complaining that he did not like working with ugly individuals. But Chanakya had made his peace with Dhana, the ruler of Magadha, and had eventually found a suitable place in its officialdom, overseeing the charities. Magadha, in what is now the northeast of India, was one of the largest of the fiefdoms that dominated ancient India.

The sage was an eccentric man, with a habit of wearing his long hair in a ponytail tied over the crown of his head, and he had a rather tactless, abrupt manner—but this was tempered by his fair-mindedness and concern for justice (something King Dhana apparently cared little about). Chanakya had a heart for the underdog. He liked to create legislation that stopped people taking advantage of women and children, or molesting their servants. He went out of his way to make sure that officials did not exploit the poor. He thought it important that the sick and infirm were cared for. So running a welfare trust was a perfect job for him. Or it had been, until that day.

What was the final straw that ended his career? No historical source tells us exactly what the issue was. But there are numerous legends about Chanakya, and one particular tradition, in which he has a fierce row with the king, appears to be a likely candidate for the argument that turned ruler and official into arch enemies.

There had been a grand reception organized for 10 leaders of the land: the guests of honor were to be the 10 top people in Pataliputra, the capital of the kingdom of Magadha. These 10 were listed as nine members of the Nanda Clan and the Master of the Vedas—the most learned professor of ancient writings. Chanakya was incensed to learn that the tenth chair had been assigned to a young man named Subandhu, a sycophant who knew almost nothing about the scriptures. Chanakya was beyond furious. He felt he had been born for that chair, which was not just a physical seat, but a symbol of rank. His fabled intelligence had first been noted when he had recited lengthy sections from the Vedas at the age of four.

So he decided to just take what was he felt rightfully his. He had marched into the room, and placed himself on the tenth throne, in front of the tenth gold plate. This probably occurred, if it happened at all, at the Nandas' royal citadel of Rajagriha.

When the royal party and Subandhu arrived, they were irritated to find their carefully laid plans upset. One of the members of the royal family, Sukalpa Nanda, angrily ordered the intruder to vacate the chair. Chanakya stayed put. He calmly explained that the seat was reserved *not* for an individual, but for the holder of the title "Master of the Vedas." Since he himself was the true Master of the Vedas, he would have the seat. If there was any dispute as to his right to hold this title, he would happily engage in literary debate and prove that he, and no other man (surely he would not have been able to resist making a sharp glance at Subandhu at this point), was entitled to that seat.

The royals ordered him to move and insulted him, with Sukalpa said to have described him as "an ugly black monkey." Chanakya replied that they may disagree with him, but should nevertheless follow his line of reasoning, since the absolute principles of *dharma* (virtuous action) had to be followed by all people, royals as well. "Furthermore, I may be black like a monkey, but scholars are noted for what is inside, not what is outside," he is quoted as replying.

This was too much. The young royals were furious at his insolence, and ordered the guards to remove him by force. "Drag him out by his ponytail," Sukalpa ordered. King Dhana Nanda declared that Chanakya was hereby stripped of his post as president of the royal welfare trust. As Chanakya continued to resist, Sukalpa lost his temper and went one step further, ordering that he be put to death. "No, please forgive him," a shocked minister named Subuddisarman interrupted.

Chanakya, rigid with fury, stepped down from the seat, his distinctive ponytail swinging. With one swift movement, he pulled the hair band from it, so that his hair fell around his shoulders. "I swear I will not retie my hair until I can re-tie it in a kingdom run by a just and wise king," he said—or words to that effect. And then he stormed out of the room.

One can picture the uncomfortable silence that must have followed Chanakya's departure. The sage's final words would have sounded like a threat. I can picture King Dhana trying to rekindle the party spirit by laughing off the official's words. After all, what sort of revenge could a single man with no weapons take?

And now, some hours later, here was Chanakya, standing in a village at the edge of the forest on the outskirts of the city of Pataliputra. Curious villagers surely stood in their doorways and looked at the lost court official who had wandered absently into their lives. Small children, I imagine, retreated behind their mothers' legs. Apparently, a group of boys looked over from their work in the fields nearby.

The man would have wandered slowly, in what we would probably today call a post-adrenalin low, past the village meeting house, and across to the path that led out of the settlement. But the way ahead was blocked by an overgrown thorn bush, taller than a man. He stopped and stared at it, apparently unsure of what to do next. He was at a crossroads, and his path ahead was blocked, literally and metaphorically.

## WHAT GOES UP...

VISHNUGUPTA CHANAKYA LIVED more than 23 centuries ago, and in truth, we know little about the details of his life. What we have is a mixture of historical data, legends, myths and stories. Yet there is surely a fair portion of trustworthy material here: relatively few of the anecdotes contain miracles and portents. None of them describe him as a tall, handsome and god-like man (standard attributes of heroes in Indian myth-making). Most are retellings of incidents in the life of a rather irascible, hot-tempered, ugly and under-sized man, and as such are likely to be rooted in actual events.

We also have his writings, which were deemed valuable and have been handed down to us in what seems to be a reasonably coherent package, albeit with signs that they have been fairly copiously edited, embellished and augmented. (The only editions that have survived until the present day were not published until several centuries after his death.)

So despite some difficulties, there is much the historian can surmise. For example, we cannot know for sure how the relationship between Chanakya and a particular family in a village on the edge of Pataliputra started, although we know it did: for that friendship changed the course of history. What is known for sure is that this wise but eccentric man was raised (and had probably been born) in Magadha in north-eastern India, with the name Vishnugupta (some say he was born in Taxila, where he went to university). He became better known under the name Chanakya, probably meaning "son of Chanak." His father was a teacher of some kind. As a boy, he had excelled at school and was sent to Taxila University on the other side of the country, in what is present-day Pakistan. This was one of the top universities in the world, and was already a legendary institution, half a millennium old by the time he arrived to attend his first lectures. People traveled from around Asia to study there, and it was a popular place for noblemen to send their sons. Indeed, it was said that one teacher had more than 100 students in his class, and every one of them was a prince of some sort.

Small, dark and wiry Chanakya, quick-thinking and sharp, had thrived at the university, and was soon invited to join the staff. But when an invasion from Greeks led by Alexander the Great caused unrest in northern India, and particularly the area around his university, Chanakya moved back across the country to the place where he had grown up, to the kingdom of Magadha.

There, his skills in logic and oratory had been recognized at the highest level, and he had been given a job in the staff of the court of the Nanda Clan, working under King Dhana. It seemed fitting: his trajectory, all his life, had been in a single direction: up.

But he had found the palace full of intrigue. The king was an unpleasant and arbitrary man, famed for his creativity in thinking up new taxes with which he could extract money from his subjects. The courtiers reacted by becoming political animals in the worst sense. No one trusted anyone else, and all continuously jockeyed for position. Chanakya had initially risen above all this—but somewhere along the line, he had probably spoken the truth too many times, been too smart, got it right too often, and had become a threat. The king had turned against him. The courtiers had raced to back their leader. The relationship had deteriorated quickly. And now, after the shocking row at the reception, Chanakya was gone for good.

And so, on that grim day, he had wandered through the streets of Pataliputra, lost in a daze—until he had found that his undirected feet had taken him to this village. Why was he here? Had he intended to come here? Or had he just wandered in this direction by accident? We learn that he was awakened from his gloomy reverie by the obstacle that blocked his path.

He stared at it. The thorn bush, I imagine, was probably some sort of saw-tooth grass clump, with pin-sharp needles at the end of each frond. It would have started off growing innocently enough at the side of the path, but would have gradually spread until it had made the track impassable. The path could not be extended the other way, although records do not tell us why: perhaps it was too steep, or there was a water course there.

Chanakya could see where people had hacked away at the bush, cutting it back. He would probably have spotted discarded piles of yellowed fronds, where villagers had slashed at the leaves. But it had been to no effect: the thorn bush had always grown back, thicker and stronger. So the path had become impassable.

I imagine this highly analytical sage considering the situation: the village; the people; the blocked path. Why had destiny, or his subconscious, led him here? Pataliputra was not a big city, and somewhere in the back of his mind, he probably knew something about this village. This was where some distant relations of the royal family lived—a rather poverty-stricken group of relatives, as was clear from the conditions of the settlement.

A light came on in his eyes. Chanakya, I imagine, would have spoken to the villagers: "That thorn bush—it is blocking the only path out of the village, correct?"

The villagers confirmed that this was true.

"So we should be rid of it."

The men, the story says, explained that they had tried cutting it down, but it always grew back. They told him how they had tried burrowing down to its roots, but they were too deep and too difficult to dig out.

Chanakya quickly struck up a relationship with the group of teenage boys who had come to stare at him. He asked them to fetch him a digging stick. One youngster, who had a rather regal manner, organized the others to get him anything he needed.

The sage started digging under the thorn bush, exposing the roots. After some heavy work, the white roots were partially exposed all the way along the bush's outer perimeter. He turned again to the villagers, continuing to direct his comments to the young man who had caught his attention before. "Get me a vessel of cane sugar toddy."

The boy, as before, relayed the message to his companions. Chanakya was intrigued by the imperious and regal child, whose nickname may well have been Peacock Boy—derived from his family name Maurya, which was said to come from the word *moyira*, the Sanskrit name of the regal Indian bird, and his noble bearing.

The container of sweet drink arrived. "Thirsty work?" I hear a villager ask, pointing to the container.

“This is not for me,” Chanakya replied, carefully emptying half the container of sugar-water along the exposed roots of the bush. The rest he sprinkled on the leaves of the plant.

It takes less than an hour before the real attack on the bush started. And this time it did not involve humanity. We see Chanakya sitting back, relaxing under the village tree, probably with another vessel of cane sugar toddy, and receiving commentaries on the progress of the battle from Peacock Boy and the other villagers.

Have you seen what happens which you spill a sugary drink on the ground in hot, lush, northeastern India? The ordinary ants arrive first. Then the soldier ants. Then the beetles. Then the flies. The sweet, sticky drink poured into the roots of the plant would soon have turned the surrounding soil into a heaving mass of insect bodies, and the sugar on the leaves would have attracted caterpillars and other leaf-eating species.

The bush, the legend says, was soon a tottering skeleton of its former self. It crashes to the ground. Peacock Boy ordered his friends to drag it away.

There was a message here. “When a thorn bush is blocking your path, you don’t fight it,” Chanakya told his audience. “You think hard about the situation. Once you have considered every option, you develop a plan of action—what we call a strategy. Then you get as many friends together as you can. And they don’t have to be big and powerful friends. They can be small. If you have enough brains, and the right friends, you can get rid of anything you want.”

The villagers nodded, grateful to him for unblocking the path.

But Chanakya had not been talking about the thorn bush.

## STARTING WITH A STRATEGY

THE EXTRAORDINARY TALE OF Chanakya's journey from power to disgrace and back to power is really a story about a struggle against impossible odds.

King Dhana had enormous power. He had a standing army, plus the ability to draft anyone he felt like conscripting. He had infantry men with armor, swords, shields and spears, and various types of bow. He had horsemen. He had war elephants. And he had thick fortifications around his palace.

In contrast, the man whom the king had made into his nemesis had only one weapon, but it was an impressive one: his brain. For Chanakya was a strategist like no other. One thousand years before Machiavelli, he sat down with a piece of palm-leaf paper and worked out a scheme—a devious, anger-fuelled, cunning, wily scheme—to oust the Nanda clan. His overriding skill was analysis: all battles, whether easy or seemingly impossible, needed detailed study, he believed. His academic background served him well in military strategizing. Once every detail of every factor was worked out, then the true facts of the situation became evident: and there were always marked differences between surface assumptions and the actual facts on the ground. *He who knew the difference had a significant advantage*. Only after one was confident that one knew all the facts, could one start to work out a strategy to attack. And a straightforward face-to-face battle was a fool's game, if one was fighting a stronger enemy. One had to employ a variety of means, obvious and unobvious, direct and indirect, straightforward and convoluted, expected and unexpected.

Chanakya was an addictive scribbler. He pulled pen and paper out of his pocket and sat down to work out exactly what challenges he had to face, and what strategies he would need to overcome them.

Problem one: King Dhana had a huge, powerful army, while Chanakya had nothing. The analysis: The king was a bad ruler, and an unpopular one. Thus he had made many enemies, including most of the populace, plus people in neighboring lands. The solution: Get them on side. The people's army is not as big as the people. Team up with other rulers, and use complex battle strategy, attacking on multiple fronts, to divert and rout his forces.

Problem two: King Dhana had royal blood, while Chanakya had none. The solution: Gather behind an alternative king, a young man with royal blood of his own, and argue that he is the "rightful" heir to the throne. Get the power of *dharma,* of virtue, on one's side.

Problem three: King Dhana, because of his big family and powerful contacts, had a deeply entrenched power base. The solution: Use religion, which was an even more deeply entrenched code of belief throughout the population. Use the fact that the rightful heir and his advisor were both Brahmins, while King Dhana was descended from a mere royal barber.

Problem four: The king's generals had good information networks that had been in place for years. The solution: Use a network of spies to make sure the rebels had at least as much information as the generals did. Generate a group of infiltrators who would deliberately release disinformation to confuse the king's men and guide them in the wrong direction.

Chanakya needed his own king. And the youngster we are calling Peacock Boy, Chandragupta Maurya, turned out to be the perfect choice. For a start, he had royal blood—and the personality to match. The Maurya family name was often found among descendants of peacock-tamers, but in this case, the young man seemed to deserve the name perfectly. We read that he acted with the grandeur of a peacock, and had risen naturally to be the leader of the young men of the village. He was brave, confident and knew how to make people listen to him. He had no kingdom, but he had the *character* of a king.

In the interests of historicity, it must be said that the story of Chanakya's meeting with Peacock Boy in the family village can never be proved to have occurred in the way tradition says it did. Scholars say that since Chanakya was a university professor at an establishment favored by young men of good families, young Chandragupta, with his royal blood, may simply have been one of his students. Another legend says that young Chandragupta actually met Alexander the Great and was inspired to become a fighter, at least partly to evict the Greeks from northwestern India.

But however Chanakya and Chandragupta initially met, the key factors of their relationship are not in doubt. They became teacher and pupil, and the things they studied had nothing to do with the school curriculum. As a professor of Taxila University, Chanakya was used to training young men rigorously. But on this occasion, he would be using his skills to prepare them for something else: to take over a major kingdom.

## HOW TO OVERCOME IMPOSSIBLE ODDS

CHANAKYA APPARENTLY ALWAYS carried a collection of notes and jottings with him. He became associated throughout Indian history with wise and offbeat aphorisms. Later in this volume, we will look at the ideas in books he eventually wrote, particularly one called *Arthashastra*. Although little known today outside India, it is a treasure trove of ideas on management and strategic techniques. But before we focus on that, we will look at the lessons we can take from the life of the man who wrote it. The wonderful thing about this sage is that he seemed to try so hard to win a measure of immortality with the books he wrote—and as with so many people who end up making history, his life itself turned out to be an object lesson in how to achieve greatness. Looking back over Chanakya's amazing bid for power, there are a number of clear lessons we can draw.

***You already have the greatest secret weapon you could possibly want.***

Chanakya, when he loosened his hair and declared war on the King Dhana Nanda, had no weapons and no army of any kind. He had nothing but confidence and determination. He had what we would call today the *right mindset*. This was enough. It was the key ingredient: it was the snowball down the mountain that starts the avalanche. If one has determination, intelligence, single-mindedness and hunger to succeed, then everything else one needs is of secondary importance.

King Dhana had the superficial trappings of success: the army and the cavalry and the swords and spears and the thick-walled palace. But he lacked the emotional focus and mental power to hold on to those trappings. He was not determined enough or smart enough—nor did he have the ability to think strategically.

How often do we sit at our desks and think: "If only we had X, we could achieve Y?" In other words, we are using our lack of a piece of equipment, big or small, as an excuse to stop us heading for our destination. If only I had a better computer, I could design a great website. If only I had space and time and a nice writing desk, I could write a great book. If only I had a small shop, I could be a brilliant retailer. If only I had a studio, I could be an artist. And the most common excuse of all: if only I had money, I could make more money.

Now I am not saying that we do not need money and equipment to succeed in business. Of course, there are many important things that we need to help us on our way. Chanakya also needed a great many things: he needed a king he could champion, and he needed armies. These are not things you find in the local corner shop.

But he didn't worry about it. He realized that these were secondary. When he made the vow to keep his hair untied until the king had been replaced, he had none of the physical things he needed: all he had was the determination to stop at nothing to achieve his goal. If you have that, you have started the journey to getting what you want. Recognize what the first step is, and get it out of the way.

Here's a quick case study: A man who had been a fitness trainer for 20 years told me that there were two types of clients who came to him. "The first sort think the first step is to go to the shop and buy vast amounts of equipment and sports gear; they look through magazines and catalogues and spend a small fortune. The second type think the first step is to get out of the house and start jogging. The second group wins hands down. The first lot has the gear. The second lot has the determination. You've just got to decide to do it—and then do it." Make the decision and set out to do it. Once you have started out on the road, you will gather the things you need on the way—or they will find you.

***To build anything great, you need a great team.***

"A single wheel cannot move anything," Chanakya wrote in the notes that became *Arthashastra*. "Leadership is possible only with assistance." This is one of the key themes of the sage's wisdom.

There was no way that Chanakya could have defeated King Dhana or any other members of the Nanda Clan on his own. He would probably have failed a hand-to-hand battle with any individual member of the family, or any of their servants. He was, after all, a weedy scholar, a nerd, a puny man abused with the nickname "monkey." Yet he wanted to overthrow the entire dynasty, a kingdom protected by a massive army. How did he do it? Initially, by knowing his own limits: he was in no position to fight any battle by himself. He realized that he had to gather around himself the right people to enable him to achieve his goals.

These are issues we all face: we all have ambitions, vague or otherwise. But most of us rarely put much strategic thought into achieving them. What are your specific aims? What exactly do you want to achieve? "Success" is not an adequate answer. "Money" is not a good answer. "Wine, women and song" is a little too general to be of use. Many business books encourage us to write down our aims and objectives. It's good advice. These are steps that should come naturally to the ambitious. We want to achieve something, so let's decide clearly what it is and give ourselves a timeline. It's necessary to have a target and a plan on how to achieve it. But the question that should follow does not come so naturally: who can you gather by your side to help you realize these ambitions?

Ambitious people tend to be confident in their own abilities—and that often means *over*-confident. We focus on our own strengths, not realizing that (a) we *all* need team members, and (b) our choice of partners will be crucial to our success. Inability to realize this is surprisingly common, even among the most active business people. To some extent, it's natural for leaders-in-waiting to shy away from team-building.

For many entrepreneurial types, control of expenses and control of profits is vital. They don't want to add staff to their payroll—especially key staff, who will have to be paid hefty chunks of money, and would have a share in the decision-making process. Ambitious types often feel they would like to do every job themselves.

You probably know the train of thought. Good people are expensive. Good people need managing. Why don't I just do it myself? I'd have to spend all my time training them, when I could do a better job—quicker, easier and a darn sight cheaper. I should do *everything* myself.

This line of argument is a tempting one, but it's almost inevitably the road to failure. There are very few business activities today that do not benefit from being done by a team. Even the smallest of corporations needs warm bodies to provide muscle, mental and physical. Imagine you have small-scale ambitions: perhaps you want to run a cookie shop that you can grow into a tiny chain, with three or four outlets in your town. You could hire a space, buy a sack of flour and get baking. But what will happen? All you would do is work yourself to death. You can see this happening all the time. Never mind ordering in the flour: the business won't thrive unless you order in the right human ingredients, too—baking staff, shop staff, someone who knows something about marketing and an accountant on the team. You need these functions covered. However small you start, any degree of success means that eventually (and probably sooner than you think) all these jobs are likely to be done by someone other than yourself. And then the most important role of all, you need to reserve for yourself: *cookie store visionary*.

The adage that "the total is more than the sum of its parts" is never truer than when engaging with the wider world, whether we are talking about business battles or actual warfare. So first, build up your team. Unless you choose very badly indeed, the total will be greater than the sum of the parts. Your project will be powered by your energy, your workmates' energy, and most of all, by the creative energy that comes from the interplay between members of the team.

*Your critics are your friends.*

This is something that King Nanda did not realize when he surrounded himself with yes-men and threw out the wisest person in the kingdom. One of the most important jobs of your team members is to disagree with you. Benjamin Franklin is one of many wise men who have made the point that our critics are our friends: they are the people who give us the information we need with which to improve ourselves. Yet human nature being what it is, this is one of the hardest lessons to learn. And even if we take it in mentally, it's difficult to internalize it to such a degree that we automatically act upon it. Yet its importance cannot be over-emphasized: having another pair of eyes, or two or three or six pairs of eyes, inspecting and criticizing our projects can only do them good. We all sneer at committee meetings and we characterize them as a big waste of time, but in reality, the process of talking through issues is almost always valuable, and frequently produces fresh ideas and refinements that turn out to be crucial to the project in hand. But it takes a good leader to lay out his plans for those under him to criticize. And it takes an even better leader to realize that the critical subordinates who make sure he is keeping on track are doing him a favor.

In Chanakya's day, long before the invention of any sort of mechanical clock, there was a group of people who performed that role: they were known as the shadow-measurers. Their job was to keep an eye on the lengthening of shadows and strike a bell to let the ruler know that another hour had passed. This was to prompt the king to keep working, and never to relax too much. It was a dangerous job, particularly if the king had a temper. "People who measure shadows and strike the hours of the day to warn their leader that he is being lax should always be respected," Chanakya wrote in *Arthashastra*.

***Spend time and effort choosing the members of your team: this is one of the most important jobs a leader can do.***

Chanakya studied the experts on this subject, and found out that there was a lot of heated discussion on this. After all, he was not just choosing team members, but a future king. Should you choose people you know? Or should you select strangers with good CVs? The sage came out with the following summary of expert views of his time:

> *"The leader," says Bháradvája, "should employ his former schoolmates as his ministers. He can trust them, because he has personal knowledge of their honesty and capacity."*
>
> *"No," says Visáláksha, "They have been his playmates, so they will have no real respect for him. He should employ people with whom he has shared secrets. People with shared intimacies are in a position where they cannot betray each other."*
>
> *"This may be true," says Parásara. "Scared that his own secrets may be revealed, the leader may follow them in their good and bad acts. He will be under the control of these people. Instead, he should employ people who have shown utter devotion to him under the most severe tests."*
>
> *"No," says Pisuna. "They may show devotion, but this is not the same as intelligence. He should appoint people who are good at finance, people who have shown good returns on investments."*
>
> *"No," says Kaunapadanta. "These people may not have the other qualities necessary for being senior ministers. The leader should employ in senior positions those whose fathers and grandfathers have taken such positions before. Their knowledge of past events and the length of their relationships as families, these things are important. Such relationships will survive difficult patches. Even out in*

*the fields, you will see that cows know which herd they belong to."*

*"No," says Vátavyádhi, "People like that can acquire complete dominion over the ruler and usurp his position. He should hire people who have newly graduated in the science of governance. They will see the leader as the leader and will show him respect."*

*"No," says the son of the female sage Báhudantí. "A man with only theoretical knowledge and no practical experience of governance is likely to mess up when faced with the actual situation. The ruler should choose as senior ministers people who come from the right backgrounds, and who have wisdom, purity of purpose, bravery and loyal feelings."*

*"This is satisfactory in all respects," says Chanakya. "For a man's ability is inferred from his capacity shown in work."*

In other words, there are a great many factors that come to mind when selecting staff. Be careful to avoid looking at only one or two, when many or all of them are important.

***To take control of a place, you need to study the lay of the land.***

When I say "place," I am thinking in physical and metaphorical terms. The place may be the inner city downtown area where you want to become a landowner. Or the place may be an intangible space: the market for medical supplies on your city, or the "real estate" in cyberspace that is the market leader in selling three-dimensional avatars.

Chanakya's background as an academic turned out to be a key factor in his new career as a military strategist. Good scholars always study all the available literature on their chosen field of study before they attempt to create anything new. They know that to add value, you need to know what's already there and then introduce fresh elements. It sounds obvious, but to many people it isn't. They produce items that have failed before, they repeat history, and they demonstrate that they have learned nothing from the past. They need to be told: You *need* to do this homework, because the devil really is in the details. Yes, we all know that good leaders need to be able to see the big picture, and to be cookie shop visionaries, as we mentioned before—but they also need to have all the available facts before them. If you are running a factory making DVD players, you need to know how to manage a manufacturing organization. And part of that responsibility includes getting to know all the detailed stuff in your area of focus. You need to know what circuit boards and other components DVD players need, who makes them, where you can get them cheaply, and how you can finish your DVD players at a cost lower than the guy in the next DVD factory. There's no substitute for knowing everything you need to know about your target area, and no excuse for anyone in business today not doing it.

***Your competitor's weaknesses are free gifts for your team.***

King Dhana had all the power. He had all the soldiers, all the weapons, all the land. He had all the toys—how could Chanakya hope to get any sort of serious challenge going against him? The opportunity was provided by the king's weaknesses: he had no interpersonal skills, so he was widely disliked. He was a bully and an over-greedy tax collector, so there was a huge body of resentment built up against him. He had enemies. This anger and hatred and resentment were big, powerful, invisible tools that were lying around, just waiting for someone to pick them up and use them.

In every industry and every sector, the same tools are lying around. If your local newspaper is badly managed and annoys everyone, you can pick up this resentment and use it to power an alternative newspaper. If the local bakery adds too much sugar and grease to every cake, start a bakery selling light, fluffy, low-calorie doughnuts. If business success makes your competitor arrogant (as it quite possibly will), market yourself as the charming alternative.

When huge, faceless food corporations seemed to have a stranglehold on the frozen dessert business in the United States in the late 1970s, a new firm called Ben and Jerry's presented itself as a cute, human alternative, and rose with meteoric success to become an icon. The company, started with US$12,000 in 1978, was sold in 2000 for US$326 million.

It's a curiosity of business that people tend to look for gaps in the market, when they can often make more money in markets that have no gaps. If there are no restaurants in community X, you can open one; but you may discover that there's a good reason why there are no restaurants in community X: no one there likes to eat out. Alternatively, you can go to community Y, where there is already a packed but poorly managed restaurant. By setting up your own rival restaurant in community Y, better managed and serving better food, you find yourself running an eatery in a place where people like to eat out, and you have a chance of stealing your rival's clientele. Yes, you'll start off with an enemy, but this can also be a good thing: the battle between the two restaurants will stir things up. Both sides will naturally increase their marketing efforts, the customers will do their own taste-tests, and the chefs will be inspired to be more creative. As a result, the market as a whole may not sunder, but may grow. But there are dangers here: you need to make sure that you are not seen as the outsider—as the "alien" intruder, stealing the market from its rightful owner. That leads us to the next point.

***The most important tool to have on your side is "right."***

People are emotional creatures. They bond with company X, but not with company Y, which actually produces better products. For some reason, they like or respect X better and think of it as more "right." They have a strong sense of what comes across as likeable and good and fair and what doesn't. They operate with their hearts more often than with their heads.

Chanakya knew that he himself would have no chance of setting up a new dynasty. His only hope was to present his candidate as the *rightful* heir to the throne. The local boy. The one chosen by God. He made much of the fact that the young man was the son of a line of Brahmins, high-class people from a priestly line, while King Dhana was descended from a hairdresser who had an affair with a queen. He knew that the true battle for the city of Pataliputra was the one for the hearts of the people not the one against the army.

To grasp your market niche firmly, you have to convince yourself, and everyone else, that you have a right to it. The subliminal message you utter must say this clearly: "I belong here, this is my space, I am one of you, and my company makes yoghurt / brews beer / makes widgets the proper way, so we have the right to be the dominant producer of yoghurt / beer / widgets in this town." It doesn't matter if someone else has a stranglehold on the market. If you have enough self-belief in your right to have that market, and you can infect other people with that belief, then the market will eventually become yours.

Chanakya believed that the people of Magadha deserved a better leader, and believed that his protégé was the right man in the right place at the right time. Once self-belief becomes contagious and spreads through a community, you have a chance of winning the toughest battle.

***The winner of a battle is the most adaptive fighter.***

Once combat started, the rebel forces had to fight against soldiers who were better equipped, better fed and who knew the battlegrounds better than they did. In a straight battle, head to head, the rebels would have lost. So instead, they fought on multiple fronts at once, and altered any strategy that did not seem to be working. They used soldiers, they used spies, they used agents who spread disinformation, and they used disloyal members of the enemy's forces.

In business, most of us are challengers. In every field, there are the dominant players, the old school people who are already established: the individuals who got there early or used heavy investment to become the market leaders. But the old Avis slogan is really true: *We're number two—we try harder*. The people who challenge the market leader are going to be more innovative. They have to be. The old leader has an entrenched position. The word "entrenched" came to the business world from the world of warfare: it indicated that one army was so well-established in the area that it was embedded in the soil, and thus almost impossible to uproot.

Well, Chanakya's two thorn bushes—the real one, and the royal one—were both dug well into the ground. And they both could only be uprooted by the most creative of means. We'll learn more about using adaptability to win later in our story.

## THE POWER OF INFORMATION

CHANAKYA REALIZED THAT young Chandragupta's rebel army, made up of disaffected locals, plus warrior tribes from around the region, simply did not have the physical strength to take on the fighters of King Dhana and his brothers. The Nanda dynasty had many powerful followers, whose loyalty had been bought and paid for by the people's taxes. So, as we noted above, he endeavored to turn King Dhana's people against him. If you don't have military strength, you use the advantages you do have; and in the case of Chanakya, it was preparation, strategy, intelligence and creativity.

There are a number of stories about the strategies Chanakya used to unseat King Dhana. The one on which I am going to dwell is the method of information manipulation that he favored. Sometimes he could be unsubtle, advocating the faking of fatal accidents—but on other occasions, he knew that one had to be as wily as possible.

It is said that the sage wanted an inside contact in the court of King Dhana. Yet he knew the dangers of approaching and bribing one of the king's men; one would never know whether one was receiving good information or being double-crossed (after all, people can be sneaky). So instead, Chanakya determined that the only way to get trustworthy data was to create his own channel to the inside. To this end, he decided that he needed two things: detailed information from someone who could penetrate the king's defenses; and a third party who could appear to be independent of the battle, and who could use the information. He commissioned a man named Indusarman to gather information about the king, his men and the palace, the story goes. The hired researcher also talked to Chandragupta and the older people in the young rebel's family, aiming to collect stories about the former royal families and the royal residences.

Indusarman, dressed as a monk, did his job well, and came back with information on the lives and loves of many of the king's associates, plus details of a major scandal, and it was a dramatic one.

Within the walls of the palace itself, there was the dead body of a Brahmin. The man was killed in a row, many years ago. The royal family, wanting to hush it up, had the body buried under the floor of a back room—the seventh room at the back corridor. The younger generation, including the current king, had been told nothing of this tale, which was almost literally a "skeleton in the closet" story.

Indusarman returned with these tales, and Chanakya had the information transferred to his most adept spy, one Jeevasiddhi: a man who had taken great pains never to be seen in public with anyone from Chanakya's side. After the spy was fully briefed, rumors were let loose in the town of Magadha. These said that a Jain monk had announced that he had a holy mission to destroy the rebels, and especially the rebel mastermind, Chanakya. A further rumor said that Chanakya was a sorcerer with evil powers of black magic.

Hearing the stories, King Dhana and his prime minister summoned the Jain monk—yes, our double agent friend Jeevasiddhi—to meet them. The prime minister was a cruel man named Kathyayana, but he was a loyal servant to the unpopular king, and was widely known, the legends say, as Rakshasa—the Demon. The spy did his best to confirm the rumors, telling the rulers that he too had magic powers, and planned to use them against his enemy Chanakya. Jeevasiddhi then proceeded to demonstrate his abilities by reeling off the memorized facts about the individuals in the king's court. King Dhana was stunned by the man's accuracy. The story goes that he offered Jeevasiddhi a thousand gold pieces to keep him on their side. But the spy agreed to co-operate at no cost, much to the mean king's delight.

Two weeks later, the friendship between the spy and the Nanda clan had grown stronger, and Jeevasiddhi found himself in the palace, walking past the seventh room at the back of the building. The spy suddenly stopped, and went into a simulated trance. "Here is the source of your problems," he said. "There is a dead Brahmin here, sending out signals to the live Brahmins who are your enemies: to Chanakya and to Chandragupta Maurya."

At first, the king and his helpers were baffled. But they trusted the spy so fully by that time that they agreed to call servants to dig up the floor of the room. When the bones of the dead Brahmin were found, the king became convinced that Jeevasiddhi had supernatural powers beyond those of any human, and pledged to follow any and all advice that he would give him. That was the signal for the spy to initiate a dirty tricks campaign. He ordered the king to withdraw the age-old custom of feeding the public Brahmin monks in the city. Reluctantly, the Nandas obeyed—despite the fact that they feared, rightly, that this would cause great resentment among the people. To maintain his reputation as a man of supernatural powers, the spy gave Dhana's children mild poisons, so that he could treat them and cure them of their ailments. This won him access to the highest level meetings. When the demon prime minister launched a midnight plan to capture and kill Chandragupta, Jeevasiddhi was present at the meeting and managed to get a message to the rebel leader so that he could save himself.

To be honest, many of the tales of the rebel spies have a little too much of the flavor of a TV mini-series to be accepted at face value by stricter historians, but they illustrate the sort of strategic thinking that Chanakya advocated in his writings. If the sage did not actually set in motion the above espionage campaign, he certainly would have used similar techniques. *Arthashastra* not only recommends using spies dressed as monks, but suggests using female spies to get into your rival's bed.

Once the information and disinformation flows were in place, a series of skirmishes got under way. To prevent this book becoming a military history, let us skim over the campaigns that followed. Suffice it to say that over a period of six to seven years, Chandragupta Maurya developed into a very able leader of the rebel forces. He and his sage enlisted powerful people who disliked King Dhana to help them. King Porus II joined the rebels, as did his brother Vairochaka and son Malayaketu and each of them brought an army of helpers with them.

With civil unrest fomenting in the city, Chanakya decreed it was time for the ultimate showdown in Pataliputra to begin. That's when things started to come unstuck. There were significant setbacks. The rebels' campaign, initially, was a failure. When the battles started, they were roundly defeated. They tried several times to attack the core of the city, where the king and his family were holed up. But the defenses were strong, and in each case, proved impenetrable.

Chanakya and Chandragupta realized that they needed to revise key elements of their plan. They had stumbled upon a truism not neatly put into words until two millennia later: no military plan survives the first battle. They realized that they had to continually go back to the beginning, reassemble the data, reanalyze it and draw up fresh strategies. But after several skirmishes had ended in painful failures for the rebels, they were running low on energy and morale. What was the new plan to be?

During this time, it is said, Chandragupta was in his tent, despairing about making a fourth attempt, when he overheard a mother talking to a child outside. The little boy was complaining that he was hungry but the *roti* the mother had just cooked was too hot to bite into.

"If you fold it over and bite the middle, it will be too hot," she said. "Just keep it open and nibble at the outside edges, which won't be so hot." The child tried it—his *ma* was right. The edges were cooler. And as he ate them, the center of the *roti* cooled down. He worked his way around it and eventually consumed it all.

*Eureka*. Chandragupta went and gave Chanakya a plan for once. They adopted this strategy, picking off the small defense units at the outer borders of the city. The border guards were easy to defeat. Only then did they move further in. Initially, the policy backfired on them: as they moved toward the center of town, the defeated troops regrouped and attacked from behind. But the rebels refined the strategy to station troops in defeated areas to prevent King Dhana's men recapturing lost territory.

Now they had a chance of winning.

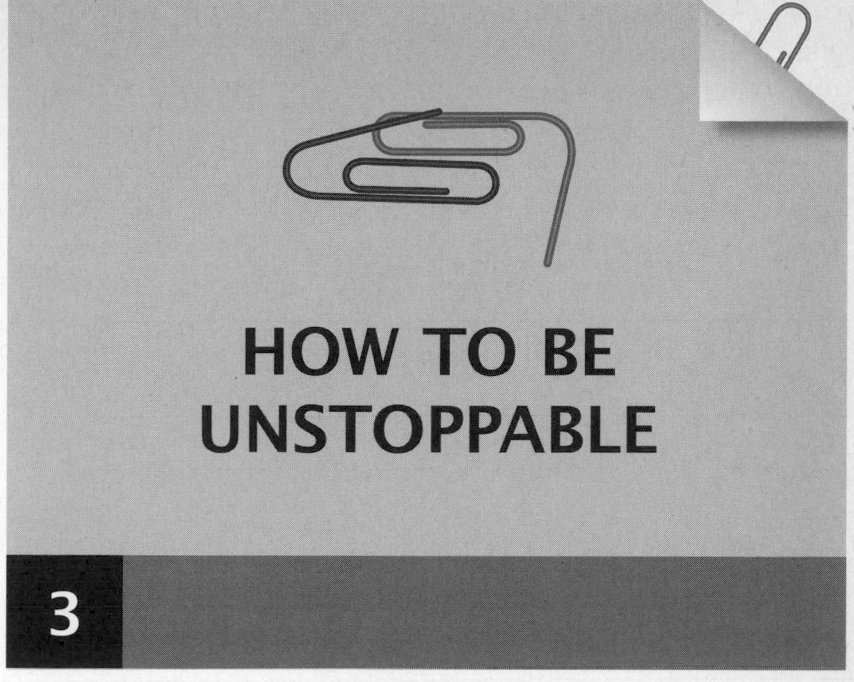

# 3 HOW TO BE UNSTOPPABLE

**A YOUNG MAN USES PRINCIPLES IN THE *ARTHASHASTRA* TO BUILD ONE OF THE BIGGEST EMPIRES IN THE WORLD—BUT HE WANTS MORE.**

## THE FINAL BATTLE

THE REVOLUTION WAS OVER. The sage Chanakya walked quickly into the palace kitchen, the vial of poison hidden in a pocket within his robes. He took a quick glance around him, to check that he was not being observed, and then he approached the food of the man whom he had made into a king: the Peacock Boy himself, Chandragupta Maurya.

There were a few kitchen staff members moving around behind him, but they were not looking in his direction. Everyone was relaxed: they were used to Chanakya's habit of "inspecting" the new ruler's dinner before it was carried to the royal table.

Some people might have thought checking the food an odd task for a royal advisor to add to his list of duties, but then Chanakya and Chandragupta had never had the normal king-and-minister relationship. Their relationship had gone through dramatic stages, from pupil and teacher, to soldier and military strategist, to king and chief advisor. The staff probably assumed that Chanakya had some sort of father-feeling for the younger man.

They would have been surprised to see what he was doing. The sage carefully tilted the bottle and allowed a drop of poison—just one drop, but enough to kill a human being—into Chandragupta's dish. Then he placed the cover back onto the plate and re-corked his bottle. Tucking it back into his secret pocket, he turned and rapidly left the room.

But we're getting ahead of ourselves. At the end of the last chapter, we left our two heroes, the sage and the rebel leader, battling toward the palace of King Dhana of the Nanda dynasty. By that time, the rebel forces had grown. As well as adding soldiers from rulers of small states around the nation, Chanakya had added the forces of his contacts from Taxila—after all, many of his former students were now in positions of power. The former general of Taxila joined the rebels. When the full rebel army was assembled, Chanakya told Chandragupta to announce that the battle would commence at a certain time on a plain just outside the city.

King Dhana ordered a platoon of soldiers to head to the site. But what the king didn't know was that the challengers had by this time posted spies within his army, and had bribed the army general. The king's army was in disarray and his command to march to the battlefield and slaughter the rebels failed to produce any appreciable result. Things were falling apart for the ruling clan. In fact, Chandragupta and Chanakya had by that time penetrated so deeply into Magadhan society that the final thrust was not so much an attack on Pataliputra, but the eruption of civil war within the city walls. In a skirmish, the King's eldest son, heir to the throne, was killed. This made the remaining Dhana loyalists worry that their royal family had no future. Popular support moved to Chandragupta and Chanakya.

In the end, there was no need to storm the palace and arrest the king. It became obvious that the battle was over. King Dhana surrendered and was sent into exile, disappearing from the pages of history. (Apparently, he was allowed to take as much wealth as he could carry himself, rather like the winner of a modern supermarket shopping competition.) Tradition says that other members of his family were executed, as Chanakya was worried that any new children born to them could be positioned as "rightful heirs to the throne"—in other words, he did not want people to use the same tactics he had used.

The usurpers then sent a message to the prime minister, Rakshasa. It said that they considered him to be serving the people of the Magadha, not the deposed king. He was invited to continue in his post. He agreed to do so, and thus the civil service remained in place for Chandragupta Maurya to be installed formally as the new king.

Standing amid the carnage, the young rebel leader was crowned the new king of Magadha. He immediately made Chanakya his chief advisor.

"We've done it," the young man says. "It's over."

The sage shakes his head. "No. Not finished yet," he replies. "I have one thing left to do."

He pulls a small band out of his pocket, gathers up his long, loose hair, and ties it in an unusual top-knot above his head. Only then does he take his seat on a chair next to the throne. "*Now* we're done," he says.

To some extent, Chanakya and Chandragupta had quietly switched places during the campaign. While the older man would always have been the teacher, the mentor, the father-figure, the dynamics would have changed: the younger man's ferocious ability to lead an army to victory would have made him the undisputed head of the empire. But the new pecking order did not cause problems between the two men; indeed, Chanakya had clearly seen it coming from the start. At no point had he harbored ambitions to become the ruler. He had known all along that his rightful place was the seat of chief advisor to the king. The bond between the two men had grown stronger, not weaker.

## ARROWS DON'T DO RIGHT ANGLES

ONCE AFFAIRS IN PATALIPUTRA were settled, Peacock Boy could have put down his sword and shield and lived out the rest of his days in luxury.

But he didn't. He had spent several years cultivating a thirst for battle, and his takeover of the Magadhan Empire failed to quench it. He had no desire to rest on his laurels. He immediately started planning a campaign to take his forces eastwards, and expand the empire in the direction of Alexander the Great.

Looking at his life, one cannot help but think he was such a driven man that he could not lower his shield and sword. He can only be pictured as a man addicted to warfare, and one can imagine how he might have justified himself: "The gods have given me this charge. They have made me Chandragupta Maurya the Unstoppable. I cannot lower my sword."

Chanakya, who had been a teacher for many years, and had studied both economics and human nature, would surely not have been in the least bit surprised by his protégé's desire to continue to expand. Indeed, I suspect he would have seen it as inevitable. If you have been involved in a steeply vertical rise to success, you are an arrow shot straight up into the sky—and that means you have to continue with your natural trajectory. You cannot just stop in mid-air. Arrows can't turn at right angles. You have velocity, you have drive, you have a direction, you have power, and that force cannot easily be suppressed. If the gods have declared that you are the Unstoppable One, then you have to be unstoppable. (People today constantly comment that it seems strange to them that elderly business leaders such as Rupert Murdoch don't retire—but they too are arrows which can't suddenly turn.)

The new ruler, Chandragupta, began a campaign to expand the borders of his empire, determined to make it as big as he could—the biggest empire India had ever seen; no, perhaps the biggest empire the world had ever seen. It appears there was something about his personality that enabled people to unite under him. He took over King Dhana's army and united it with his own. His fellow fighters, from the hill tribes, were also happy to be counted among his cohorts—or too scared of him to resist his invitation.

Within a few years of his takeover of the Magadhan Empire, Chandragupta's army grew to massive proportions. He had an astonishing 600,000 soldiers, records claim. (This is more than 10 times the size of the army of Alexander the Great, which stood at about 40,000 men.) He also had 9,000 war elephants.

Having conquered much of what we know now as northern India, Chandragupta set his sights on bigger prey: the area that Alexander the Great had taken over, now the land of five rivers known as Punjab, but also spelled as Panjab. (*Panj* means five, *ab* means waters, so the land of five rivers is Punjab). Chandragupta first rid the capital Taxila of Greek troops—with Chanakya's contacts and inside knowledge of the place, it was a relatively easy target. Seleucus I, a Greek leader (Alexander being dead by this time), tried to recapture the northwestern part of India in 305 BCE. The Magadhan ruler defeated him, but decided that he was a powerful enemy who would be better to have as a partner. Chandragupta joined the families together by accepting Seleucus's daughter in marriage—and he gave the Greek leader 500 war elephants in exchange.

The Magadhan Empire's capital Pataliputra was rebuilt and turned into a big city ruled from a walled compound that had 570 towers. The Greek writer Megasthenes moved into Chandragupta's court to record the wonders of the powerful super-kingdom: no longer a state ruled by a king, but a great empire ruled by a true emperor. Megasthenes was a sort of foreign correspondent, akin to the traveling feature-writers we get in our newspapers today. He wrote home about the marvels of India, including sheep-wool that grew by itself on trees without the use of sheep (cotton trees); and a magical reed that produced the most delicious drink (what we know today as sugarcane).

Indeed, it has been the combination of Greek, Roman and Indian sources that have enabled modern historians to get a grasp of Chandragupta's reign. For years, scholars examined Greek records, including surviving fragments from Megasthenes, which tell the story of a ruler named Sandrokottus, but it wasn't until 1793 that a brilliant Orientalist named Sir William Jones made the link between that name (on one occasion spelled "Sandrakoptus") and Indian records of the man called Chandragupta.

Between 321 and 297 BCE, the Magadhan Empire became unquestionably the main power base of ancient India. But it wasn't all about fighting. This was an interesting period for another reason: two faiths had sprung up in the same part of India, and were growing steadily. There was a tribe of wandering monks known as the followers of the Awakened (in Sanskrit: the people of the *Buddha*), and there were the disciples of Mahavira Nataputta, who had founded the Jain movement, which focused on extreme respect for sentient life. The Buddha preached enlightenment.

The Jains went around naked, for fear that clothing may trap or hurt tiny insects, and they swept the road ahead of them with long-handled brushes as they walked. At that time, both these faiths were relatively new, with their recently deceased founders retained in the living memory of the older members. It was a lively and creative time in India.



## THE MAN WITH EVERYTHING

THEN CAME THE POISONING. Chanakya the kingmaker was pleased with himself. His protégé was now the ruler of a huge empire that covered almost the entire top half of ancient India. It's probably a simplification to say that with Chanakya's brain and Chandragupta's brawn, they had created an unstoppable force, but that's the way that the story of the two partners is understood in India. Certainly the king comes across as highly intelligent in his own right.

But the royal advisor remained as suspicious and wily as ever. He assumed that others would use the same tricks he did. So he searched for spies everywhere. He made sure that he had more sources of information than anyone else. And he looked out for ways that challengers might infiltrate the palace.

Then he had a worrying idea. Had he wanted to overthrow Chandragupta, he would have infiltrated the palace as a servant, and then poisoned the emperor's food. Anticipating the development of vaccines, Chanakya realized that ingesting small amounts of certain types of poison would likely make the body grow immune to that substance. He wanted Chandragupta to be indestructible—and that included the quality of being immune to poison. So every day, Chanakya added a tiny portion of a lethal poison to the emperor's food, the story goes. As the days wore on, and Chandragupta seemed unaffected by the dose,

Chanakya increased the amount—until he was putting a deadly dose of poison into the royal meal.

That evening, Chandragupta's wife Durdha, heavily pregnant and ravenous, stepped into the dining chamber as her lord was eating. "That smells wonderful," she said.

"You have to eat for two," said Chandragupta, and passed her the dish.

She died that night.

The more fanciful legends record that Chanakya grabbed a knife, expertly opened her belly and rescued the child. The baby had the drop of poison miraculously positioned on his forehead and was given the name Bindusara, *binda* meaning drop. Clearly, this ending is an invented hero-myth, but the attempt to make the emperor immune to poison may be rooted in events, and it is known that Chandragupta did have a child named Bindusara, who would eventually take over the kingdom.

Now that the land was enjoying a period of relative peace, Chanakya apparently took time to assemble his notes and publish a book. He wrote *Arthashastra*, one of the greatest treatises on economics, politics and warfare ever produced. Or at least he began it. Scholars believe the version that we have today dates from about the second century CE, and it is likely to be a compendium of the thoughts of Chanakya and those of his followers, or sages with similar interests. But the surviving scraps of work from the Greek foreign correspondent Megasthenes paint a picture of a tough, bureaucratic government: suggesting that some of Chanakya's thoughts in the *Arthashastra* were being put to practical use as soon as they were written.

The sage wrote about the importance of training for leaders, and how self-discipline was the key. "You may own every single thing in all four quarters of the world—but if you don't have self-control, you have nothing and will come to a swift end," he wrote. There were two kinds of discipline:

inborn and acquired. You need both, as instruction and training can only benefit people who already have a measure of self-discipline, he wrote. People who want to learn must have certain attributes: obedience to the teacher; a desire and the ability to learn; capacity to remember what is taught; and the ability to understand what they have heard, to reflect upon the material, and to make inferences from it.

Chandragupta must have been a good student. The achievements of the Peacock Emperor were staggering. His empire not only encompassed north India (which had the Himalayas as its natural boundary), but included all of what is now Pakistan, plus significant parts of Iran and Afghanistan. In an eastwardly direction, he had conquered northeastern India, including what is now Assam. Some scholars believe an inscription in modern-day Orissa indicates that that eastern part of India was also included in the empire. India, for the first time, stretched from one great sea to another—from the Bay of Bengal to the Arabian Sea. No one actually knows how far south the empire extended, although it is worth pointing out that Chandragupta spent his last days in Karnataka, which is a long way toward the south.

But the unstoppable fighter was not happy. He had everything any man of his generation could have ever wanted: one of the world's largest empires, wealth beyond counting, wives and children, and the respect of his people.

But there was something else he needed. And when he announced what it was, his people were shocked.

## THE WORLD'S FIRST MANAGEMENT HANDBOOK

IN 1904, A PANDIT (a term for a learned man, sometimes spelled *pundit*) walked into a library in Mysore, India. He handed over an ancient pile of palm leaf pages and then left. He did not leave his name or any contact details. The librarian realized that he had been given some sort of old book, but he could not have imagined just how old it was.

This was *Arthashastra*, Chanakya's book of wisdom—and it was the only copy. Historians had known that a book with such a title existed because it had been quoted by other writers—but they had never seen a copy. Although the edition given to the library was believed to date back to the second century CE, there is no reason to doubt that at least some of the material in it dates back to the author to whom it is attributed: the sage Chanakya, writing under his formal name of Kautilya.

A *shastra* is a scientific treatise, or a textbook. *Artha* is a Sanskrit word we are going to come across on many occasions in this volume, so let us consider its meaning carefully. It is often translated as *wealth*, although the Indian word does not have the associations, positive and negative, that the English equivalent has. For example, a spiritual leader speaking in English would be unlikely to trumpet the glorious importance of being stinking rich. But in India, it would not have been seen as a bad thing for such a person to say that *artha* is a factor important in everyone's life. In this sense, *artha* can be seen as "material possessions." Except for the most austere ascetic, we all have possessions, and it is not seen as wrong to acknowledge this. At the same time, *artha* can be used as a word for "riches," but in a much wider sense than the English word. *Artha* implies the whole physical system of possessions in a society: thus it is sometimes translated as "economics." And it also means "meaning."

The title *Arthashastra* has been translated as *The Science of Economics*, *The Handbook of Polity*, and so on. But the book focuses on all the areas surrounding statecraft, incorporating economics and other aspects of civic structure, such as politics. It moves from these sectors to cover the entire field of the legal and bureaucratic framework for good governance, as well as providing opinions and general information on fields as far apart as animal husbandry and mining. "The Science of Governing" might be a more accurate translation.

Some scholars say that textual analysis indicates that the material comes from more than one author. And certainly, the style of writing—the book is largely a list of tightly written aphorisms—does not come across as the work of an academic author, but is more like a compilation of the thoughts of a sage, or several sages. This becomes more apparent in the later volumes. But given the age of the document, it is entirely possible that other hands had contributed to it to some extent. Furthermore, we can get over this point by taking the work as authored by Chanakya and "the school of Chanakya"—his followers, disciples and fans. But to anyone who reads it, there are a number of places where the personality of the author shines through: an intelligent, sharp man who vacillates between thundering about the importance of behaving correctly toward the poor, and recommending devious ways of defeating enemies: it sounds very much like what we know of Vishnugupta Chanakya.

The sage apparently used his alternative name Kautilya when he wrote the book, probably for religious reasons. It is believed to have been his *gotra* name, meaning a name that signified which patriarchal clan he belonged to. So the volume was released as *Kautilya's Arthashastra*. Although it is bureaucratic and nit-picking in many ways, there is much wisdom there that must have been refreshing to people who had suffered under King Dhana, and Chanakya's thoughts on leadership must have made a welcome change. With an example of a bad ruler right in front of him, the sage had received from King Dhana a series of practical lessons in How Not to Lead. In contrast, the new royal advisor was determined to make absolutely sure that the king he had created would be gloriously successful. So he painted a word picture of what he believed was the ideal ruler. He wrote:

*A ruler finds happiness in the happiness of the people he is ruling,*
*And he finds welfare in their welfare.*
*Things which delight him, he will not necessarily consider good;*
*But instead, whatever pleases his subjects—those things will he consider beneficial to himself.*

This was an extraordinary line of thought in that day and age. Kings were kings, and servants were servants; the idea of a servant king did not come naturally (although it did exist among other thinkers—look at the Jewish *Book of Isaiah*, for example). And although he lived in a period during which the king and his family had absolute power, Chanakya believed that they also had absolute obligations, thanks to the concept of *dharma*. Often translated as "virtue," the word *dharma* implies righteousness that becomes action: the virtuous person's duty, if you like. So he listed a great deal of items of welfare in his list of the king's duties. During famines, it was the ruler's duty to redistribute the wealth, he said. Communities were bounded together by collective ethics.

This train of logic is precisely reflected in the way good leaders should manage organizations today, whether commercial or otherwise. The leader needs to become a servant. While many companies are identified strongly with one individual or another (think of Richard Branson at Virgin Group, or Bill Gates at Microsoft Corp.), there comes a point at which the bosses need to minister to the staff below them, and have their needs uppermost in their minds. When Richard Branson started Virgin Records, the tiny company (a record shop in London) served him. But once it started to become a group of individuals, the tables turned. Suddenly he found himself with an enormous amount of responsibility: hundreds, and then thousands, of people depended on him for their livelihood. Branson regularly acknowledges this fact, and it is one of the strands of personality that makes him one of the most popular business leaders today. Organizations become many-headed creatures, hydras if you like, and need management that acknowledges this reality.

This is a crucial step, yet it is an attitudinal change that you will not find written into any business manuals. There is no rule that says: *When you have five/25/500 staff, you become the servant as well as the leader*. Nevertheless, it is in the handling of this intangible change that leaders win respect or lose it. Think about the organization of which you are a part. Do you compartmentalize your job? Do you just make sure you come in, do your bit, and then leave? Or do you act as part of a team? Are you emotionally and mentally aware that you have responsibilities for everyone else in the organization—those under you, and those alongside you?

Chanakya knew that communities were indelibly interconnected; they were like single entities. His book tells us to think of a group as a person: a man's finger and his ear are located at different parts of the body; but if you hurt either one of them, the pain is felt by the entire body.

Today, leaders of companies have useful little things called human resources departments to take care of their responsibilities to their staff. Why worry when you can pay someone else to worry for you? But Chanakya knew that the relationship between a leader and his people had to run deeper than that. *"Whatever pleases his subjects—those things will he consider beneficial to himself."* It's not the extent of his personal shares that will thrill the true leader; it is the extent of the stock options he or she gives away to the staff.

> *The source of wealth is activity,* he wrote. *Lack of activity brings about material distress. In the absence of activity,*

*current prosperity will disappear and there will be no future growth.*

Chanakya was an early identifier of the key traits of capitalism, and noticed how concentrated free trade generated wealth for a community. Centuries before the great economists wrote their classic tomes, he pointed out that you could foretell the fortunes of a place by whether high, concentrated levels of trade were present, and whether the levels were escalating or falling.

*Movement* of goods, services, ideas and entertainment: that's where success lies. It is not of the slightest use to build a better mousetrap, or compose the perfect symphony, or design the ideal chair, if what you create does not circulate. "The source of wealth is activity." Movement is the key to business success. Only when goods are transferred from one pair of hands to another is wealth created.

It was obvious to him such a long time ago, but it is astonishing how often we still make the mistake today. We focus 90% of our energy into building up and refining the item that we think is going to make our fortune. Yet, unless there is a market for it, and a first class distribution channel to get it to the market, we are wasting our time. It would be better to spend 80% of our time perfecting a distribution method and 20% on the product that will be distributed, than the other way around.

One of the most common areas in which people make this mistake is in the publishing industry. Would-be authors come up with thoughts about what they want to write. And then they set aside a year or two and start pouring out the words. But the sad truth is that what they want to write is not the issue. What the market wants to read is the relevant fact—those are the books that are going to be printed and distributed and sold. The two need to match, or the work will never be published and succeed.

The same truism works for other industries. Anyone who creates anything, be it a product or a service or anything else, must step out of his shoes as a producer and take a walk in the shoes of the potential buyer. Only then is there a chance that the business will succeed. So stop thinking about the quality of the product or service that you are offering, and start thinking about distribution channels and marketing. It is activity that generates cash.

***If fights break out at the top of an organization, everyone stands to get hurt.***

Chanakya wrote that there was great harm when people quarreled—although the cunning sage could not resist adding that the head of an organization could sometimes benefit if people lower down fought among themselves: squabbling lieutenants have their eyes on each other, instead of looking lustfully at the general's chair, you see. But he warned that internal strife at the top was a very bad thing. If there was enmity at the top—among the royals and their prime ministers and presidents (we can think of it today as CEOs, directors and board members),—then there was a serious risk of the whole organization suffering major damage.

But what if there is strife in your rival's company? That's the time to take advantage. A small rift in the boardroom of a firm can make a big opportunity for a challenger to move in and mark out territory for himself. What boardroom battles mean is that the boundaries have become loose—and the smart player uses this knowledge to his advantage. A single fight in a boardroom can cut a company into two halves. Make an offer to hire one of the disgruntled partners of your rival: the inside knowledge you gain might prove invaluable. But tread carefully. The partner may be being kicked out because he is incompetent or troublesome—make sure you have done the research before you sign the contract.

*Arthashastra* features many examples of bite-sized wisdom on leadership. One of the overriding themes is that the key element vital for being a good boss is self-control, it says. Restrain your carnal appetite, Chanakya wrote. Lust should be avoided "even in your dreams." Not for him the permissive world, where idle titillation is considered an acceptable part of life. Vices are caused by ignorance and lack of discipline, he argued. An uneducated person doesn't realize that his vices have negative consequences for him.

The oft-quoted modern principle that "a person should be allowed to do anything he likes to himself provided he does not hurt others" would be seen as foolishness in ancient India. Every human being is an integral part of society. Damage yourself and you damage the society. Today, we act as if human beings live on individual islands. But in the past, they knew the truth. Humans constantly interacted with each other. Human society was more like a complex and delicately balanced dance. If one person has no self-control and damages himself, he ends up spoiling the dance for everyone.

Like Vatsyayana, who wrote the *Kama Sutra*, Chanakya divided life into three areas: *artha, dharma* and *kama*—virtuous action, material possessions and sensual pleasures. "These three are inter-dependent on each other," he wrote. "Any one of these, enjoyed to an excess, hurts not only the other two, but also itself."

Damaging yourself is not an option. You are too important. You do not have freedom to do this. And this is particularly true for senior people—for managers and CEOs. Leaders are models for the people under them. "If the leader is energetic, his people will be equally energetic," he wrote. "If he is slack in performing his duties, the people will also be lax—and they will thus consume his wealth."

Chanakya's *Arthashastra* included a detailed plan on how to be the perfect boss. The word he used for leader was *rajarishi* (a good ruler). This is useful advice for modern business chiefs. A good leader, Chanakya wrote:

1. Has self-control, and in particular is in control of his carnal desires.
2. Cultivates his intellect by associating with people who are older and wiser.
3. Keeps his eyes open everywhere by making use of spies.
4. Is always active in promoting the security and welfare of his people.
5. Makes sure his people observe *dharma* (act virtuously) by setting a personal example.
6. Improves his own discipline by continuous learning in all branches of knowledge.
7. Endears himself to his people by enriching them and doing good to them.
8. Keeps away from other people's spouses.
9. Does not covet other people's property.
10. Practices *ahimsa* (non-violence towards all living things).
11. Avoids daydreaming, capriciousness, falsehood and extravagance
12. Avoids association with harmful persons, and indulgence in harmful activities.

It's a list of useful guidelines, and overlaps with the Ten Commandments of Moses at some points. Let's look at some of these guidelines in more detail.

***Recognize that your most important possession is your self-control, particularly the ability to resist carnal temptations.***

Talking about self-control and personal discipline and resisting carnal temptation comes across as ludicrously old-fashioned today. Yet why should it be? Life is short. Sure you can while away a day by web-surfing at your desk or forwarding idle joke emails or vegging out occasionally. But you have to do it in the full knowledge that once that day is gone, it's gone: you will never have it back. And if you can blow a day this week, it's going to be that much harder to resist wasting a day next week. If it becomes a habit, we'll find ourselves on a long road downhill. Discipline is a bad word today. Yet for Chanakya, it was the very foundation of the good leader's personality.

I knew a senior rural journalist who decided to treat himself to a couple of pints of beer one lunchtime, even though his colleagues argued that one shouldn't take alcohol during working hours. It quickly became a habit. It was a small sin, but kept him cheerful, he argued. He was stopped by the police one afternoon while he was driving on assignment. He had to undergo a breathalyzer test, which he failed, and he lost his driving license. As a rural reporter covering a large patch, he became unable to continue in his career. A little loss of self-control caused him to lose his livelihood.

Now I don't mean to suggest that we shouldn't stop and smell the coffee occasionally, or have a glass of something stronger. Of course we should have a balanced day, with healthy breaks and reasonable downtime periods. But indolence and self-indulgence, once we give in to them, tend to escalate in size and scale: and they inevitably become the enemy of our long-term goals. And this doesn't just apply to temptations of the body: anything that distracts you from your goal is bad news.

Another example: I knew a young woman who was a hot-shot saleswoman. But then she got into the habit of spending the time between appointments window-shopping. Then she started scheduling her appointments so that they gave her an hour free in areas known for their boutiques. Then she started returning to the office after appointments laden with shopping bags. The center and focus of her working day changed. It wasn't long before there was very little difference between her workdays and her weekends. She shopped the whole week through. She became a spender; the very opposite of a saleswoman. She lost the fire that had made her a top saleswoman and found herself demotivated and distracted. She suddenly stopped achieving her sales targets and had to find a new job. She'd been tripped up by her own lack of personal discipline.

***Surround yourself with people older than you are. People with experience are an invaluable intellectual asset.***

This precept of Chanakya's is another one that is widely ignored today. Older people are "let go" first when companies are downsized. Human resources managers characterize them as more expensive than younger staff members, and with bigger potential healthcare costs. Then there's the issue of image. People like their companies to look hot and hip, and that means having a great many juniors in every position. I've been taken on tours of offices by CEOs who boast about how low the average age of their staff is. This is madness. One can certainly boast about the youth of one's aircraft fleet. But to trumpet the lack of experience and wisdom in one's staff is to make oneself look foolish.

Chanakya knew that having a large number of older staff hugely increased the knowledge base and decreased the chances of the organization going off track. It was vital, he believed, to have age and experience right in the offices of the leader, or as close at hand as possible. I recall an incident in which a newspaper printing press broke down. It was the early hours of the morning. The paper had to be printed and delivered. What could be done? While younger staff members were going through the trouble-shooting section of the manual, an older man recalled that the same thing had happened 15 years earlier: and what's more, he remembered how to fix it. He told them to pull that lever, hold down that button, and kick that panel. The machine started working again. The solution was something that was not in the manual. Having spent 15 years in intimate contact with that particular machine, the old man knew more than whoever had built the machine and written the instruction book.

Are there any old hands in your company? Is anyone older than you? Many managers don't like having older people around for another reason: it subliminally upsets the "natural order" of things. It means there are people who have seniority in terms of years, but who are not at the top of the ladder in the office. It doesn't feel right and the personal dynamics can be awkward. Yet older people have so much value that it is important to get over this obstacle. Just because they are older than you does not mean that they are lusting for your job. Chanakya knew his place: he was the wise old owl who gave advice to the emperor. The emperor was the warrior who used his sword to change the world. They could not change places, nor would either have wanted to.

What if there is no one in your office with a great deal of experience in the field? You may need help from outside—which takes us to the next point.

***Keep your eyes open and make sure you have many informers who are quite literally looking out for you.***

Sources of information are a key to business success these days. And I don't just mean reading the industry newspaper or website for your sector. That's just the start of it. Make sure you personally know many, many people in your area of business. If you are in the TV business, make sure you check in regularly with the government's TV regulators, the head of the broadcasting authority, the people in the TV workers association, and even the people working in digital media in university research departments. They are all contacts who are likely to be crucial to your success. Today, with the Internet linking everyone's computer, with television monitors springing up everywhere, and with youngsters using websites to create huge fan-bases for themselves, trends evolve faster than ever. Without knowing what is going on in your industry, you will be left behind. Have a network of people whom you contact regularly. Stick their phone numbers on your computer to remind yourself to take them to lunch at frequent intervals. Drop them an email from time to time just to keep the relationship fresh. Organize an industry get-together for lunch once a month. Set up your own industry newsletter. Get yourself into a position where nothing significant can happen in your sector without you knowing about it—first.

Chanakya believed in what we would today call "industrial espionage." He also believed in dirty tricks. In business today, we have to stick to higher standards, but the principle that the person with the right information is likely to be the winner, still stands true.

***A good leader makes sure his people observe dharma (or act virtuously) by setting a personal example.***

I want to highlight this one, because it is so rarely practiced today. All around us we see business leaders stooping as low as is legally possible. Lawyers are hired by firms not to help them stay within the law, but to find loopholes through which they can step over the line. Business leaders think themselves to be smart if they can steal a march on their rivals by doing something that regulators have not yet forbidden. Yet these same companies are baffled as to why their employees are constantly stealing office supplies, sabotaging projects, or allowing themselves to be poached by rivals.

These bosses don't link their own unethical behavior with the rising costs of employee misbehavior or the amount of so-called "damaged in transit" goods listed at their firm's transport depot. They don't realize that the more tricks they try in the boardroom to enrich themselves, the more tricks employees down the line will try to enrich themselves. And why shouldn't they? If the boss is clearly out for himself, so will the staff be. We'll look more at business ethics later in this book.

***Continue to educate yourself in all branches of knowledge.***

Two thousand years before the phrase "life-long learning" became a trendy line to encourage adults to re-enter education, Chanakya was advising leaders-to-be to never stop being students. It's not just about mastering facts: it's about having an attitude of being open to receive from others, to share in other people's discoveries, and to be a channel with a two-way valve. Furthermore, setting aside time to learn has two important benefits: first, you exercise your brain in ways that will increase your creativity; and second, you will be going through a personal growth process just as your company goes through its growth process. If your skills are expanding, so will your performance and your firm's performance.

***Make sure you endear yourself to your people by enriching them, not just yourself.***

Someone tells you that your staff is paid 2% more than other employees in the same industry sector. How do you react?

Unfortunately, many business leaders today would react the same way: they would put the human resources manager on the carpet and berate her or him. How could you let the company get into this state? We need to be competitive in every way. We have a duty to our shareholders to pay market rates and not a cent more. How soon can we freeze salaries, or, even better, implement an across-the-board pay cut?

This is the common reaction, but it is not the right one. The correct reaction is to look at the company's profit figures, dividend pay-outs and the rate of growth. If the company is rapidly losing money, then you may have to examine the payroll. But if it is making money or expanding successfully, then what is really happening is this: the company is growing, and the staff is sharing in its growth. You are not just enriching yourself, but enriching the whole family. You are doing the right thing.

## LESSONS FROM A LEADER

***The key indicator of success is not the quality of a product or service, but the velocity of its growth.***

People in creative or innovative businesses often spend their lives in a state of frustration. They have written a screenplay or designed a piece of software, and they are struggling to get the marketing people at their agency or broking house, the ones wearing suits, to take an interest. We've done the hard work, they seem to be saying: all you have to do is sell it. Yet one cannot help but feel sorry for the poor agent: there seem to be so many people doing creative, inventive things and so few people standing around with piles of money to invest in them.

Whether it is screenplays or software or song composition, these are all highly competitive markets, and selling items that you can't eat or drive or sit on and that have no clear, tangible worth, can be difficult. Agents have it tough. When you know a filmmaker has 5,000 scripts on his desk, several of which are from your screenwriters, how can you phone him up and tell him to take yet another and another and another? In fact, there are investors out there. There are people who want your piece of software or your screenplay. How do you get them on side?

The answer lies in the hands of the creator of the item in question: make sure your product has *velocity*. Make sure it is hot and happening, even on a small scale. Ensure that the investor gets the feeling that your project has energy, that it has legs, and that it is already on the move. Sell 5,000 copies by hand from the back of a truck. Make demo copies that you give away at school fairs. Get it on top of the bestsellers' list, even if it's just the bestsellers' list for a small town.

If you were a venture capitalist, which of the following two propositions would you find more attractive?

(a) Please, please, please have a look at my project. I don't know who else to turn to and I need the money.

(b) My project is hot and happening and about to go ballistic. I might be able to cut you in, but no promises.

Of course, any investor would rather take a cut of a deal that appears to be on a roll than pick up a project that has no track record of any kind. Yet venture capitalists, publishers, film houses, software brokers and other agents constantly hear the first message; rarely the second. So remember: it's not about the product; it's about the velocity. Or think of it this way: investors will only hitch a ride on a moving vehicle.

*Tie powerful people into your team by making wise exchanges.*

When Chandragupta went to war with Greek leader Seleucus I, the outcome was unclear. The Magadhan emperor won most of the land in the deal, but the two foes did not stay enemies. Chandragupta took Seleucus's daughter into his family (although we don't know whether she became his wife or the wife of one of his sons). Also, he gave the Greek leader 500 war elephants, which he went on to use to great effect in battles unrelated to India.

We all meet people who can help us from time to time. Don't be scared of them. Hitch your wagon to theirs, and offer to give them whatever help you can in return. While a class system exists to some extent in every society, people with good social skills have an enormous advantage. If you can engage a powerful person on your side, it can make a huge difference to your business. If it is not inappropriate, give them a gift. (But not something expensive—Chanakya says "giving a valuable gift to a rich man is like rain falling into the sea.") Accept gifts you are offered from them. The high-energy team you have built will become even stronger if you have powerful strategic partners.

*The ultimate prize may not be what people think it is.*

What did Chandragupta Maurya want? He was head of the one of the biggest empires on earth, and had everything money could buy. He also had friends and family who loved him. But he felt strongly that neither material goods nor family attachments gave him the fulfillment he wanted. He wanted something else.

## THE MAN WHO GAVE AWAY THE WORLD

THE MAN WHO HAD everything wanted nothing.

I'm not using that phrase in the sense that he had everything he wanted, nor do I mean that he wanted to have as little as a person could possibly have and survive. No, he wanted to have nothing at all. He wanted to have no home, no friends, no family, no possessions, no food, no drink, absolutely nothing—no life-force throbbing through his veins, no *life*. He wanted to be free of everything. If all the possessions in the world could not satisfy him, he had decided to go to the opposite extreme. He wanted fulfillment, and he became convinced that ending his life with a journey inward, toward his soul, was the way to find it.

He began studying Jainism, the new faith that had been sweeping through the country in the past few decades, and he quickly became an adherent of the most extreme form of the faith. As mentioned earlier, Buddhism and Jainism were in their infancy in India at the time, and teachers of the two codes of belief were highly active, traveling from city to city giving talks about their faiths.

And so Chandragupta Maurya gave it all away. His palace, his soldiers, his crown, everything he owned, he passed to family and friends. Despite the violence he had needed to use to build his massive empire, India was at peace. There was no significant unrest when he abdicated from the throne, passing it on to his son Bindusara.

Although Bindusara lacked the charisma of his father, he appeared capable of holding things together, and possibly even continuing the expansion of the kingdom.

But Chandragupta no longer cared. He had detached himself from everything: physical and emotional needs no longer had any effect on him. Then he dressed himself in the humblest sackcloth and joined a group of the most austere ascetics on the planet. One can barely understand how his mind could have worked at this time, or what his friends and family thought about his decision. But no one tried to stop him. After all, this Maurya was the unstoppable. If he wanted to do anything, he just did it.

Chandragupta became a disciple of a Jain saint called Acharya Bhadrabahu, who was the eighth, and by some accounts, the last living direct pupil of Mahavira Nataputta, the founder of Jainism. The emperor and a group of other Jains traveled south to Karnataka and settled on an isolated piece of land that had two mountains with a river running between them. They lived in the most humble circumstances in a cave in a place called Sravanabelgola, and built temples and abstract statues. (The cave is still there, and it appears that almost nothing has changed for more than 2,000 years.)

The former ruler embraced a teaching called *sallekhana*, a practice of voluntarily embracing holy death through fasting. Jainism, like other religions, considers suicide to be sinful and wrong. However, *sallekhana* is categorized differently. Self-starvation was different, in that it was simply an acknowledgment of the built-in obsolescence of the human body. It was not seen as an active act of suicide, but merely the refusal to prolong the wait for inevitable death.

The Jain saint would have instructed Chandragupta to repent for all misdoings, all violent acts, all falsehoods uttered, all sensualities enjoyed and all worldly belongings acquired. Then the emperor would have been told to detach himself from all things in life, including food and water. In committing *sallekhana*, Chandragupta would have been warned that the noble act of starving to death would be null and void if it were done for wrong purposes, such as to acquire reputation among human beings; to acquire divinity; to acquire personal popularity; or to hasten death in order to escape pain or suffering. Instead, it was to be embraced as a way of fulfilling one's destiny by voluntarily leaving one's earthly body and becoming part of the immortal firmament.

Then the emperor would have been told to begin to meditate. Chandragupta was as unstoppable in this aim as he had been in all other things. He sat quietly in the cave in Karnataka, and starved himself to death. And in view of the fact that he is one of the few people of that era whose name is still remembered, he did achieve a measure of immortality.

## A VIOLENT END

AND WHAT HAPPENED to his old friend and mentor, the man with many names, the man born as Vishnugupta, but known as Chanakya, and who became the author Kautilya? He did a lot more writing and editing—and presumably cultivating his school of disciples who compiled the writings. There are three books bearing his name in circulation these days. In addition to *Arthashastra,* which had an economics and governance theme, there was *Nitishastra,* which was a more general compendium of aphorisms of life, and *Chanakyashastra,* which was a general collection of his thoughts.

These are all patchy works, varying greatly in style, and sections of them were clearly written by other people "from the school of Chanakya" rather than from the man himself. Yet they are well worth reading, for the offbeat and often provocative ideas in them. Often, they have something of the flavor of Zen thought, which we associate with a much later form of Chinese Buddhism. Some people think the lack of violence in them signifies that this was not written by the same person who wrote *Arthashastra*. But it could equally well be argued that he mellowed a little as he got older. To give you a flavor of his later works, here are some of the ideas for living from *Nitishastra*:



*When you are on the road,*
*don't stop for a single day in a town*
*where you do not find the following five things:*
*a rich man,*
*a priest who knows his scriptures,*
*a governor,*
*a river*
*and a doctor.*

*He who gives up what is imperishable*
*for that which is perishable, loses both.*

*If gold has fallen into a dung heap, you pick it up;*
*so be willing to find wisdom from the mouths of the low class.*

*Sometimes a jug of poison*
*has a layer of milk floating on top.*

*Scrutiny drives out fear.*

*There is no disease like lust,*
*no enemy like infatuation,*
*no fire like anger,*
*and no happiness like spiritual wisdom.*

*Time perfects all living beings*
*but it also kills them.*

*When all things are asleep,*
*time alone is awake.*

*It is said there is a ruby in every mountain,*
*a pearl in the head of every elephant,*
*a sadhu in every town*
*and a sandalwood tree in every forest;*
*but it is not so.*

*Parents who do not educate their children*
*are their enemies.*

*He who gives up being timid in handling money,*
*in acquiring knowledge,*
*in eating*
*and in business,*
*becomes happy.*

*A single withered tree set alight*
*can destroy a whole forest.*

*Always feel satisfied if you have these three things:*
*a spouse of your own;*
*enough food to eat;*
*payment for honest effort.*
*Never be satisfied with the amount you have of these*
*three things:*
*knowledge;*
*spirituality;*
*good works.*

*An elephant is controlled by a tiny stick.*
*Darkness is banished by a little candle.*

*A hill can be ravaged by a single lightning bolt.*
*Power counts, not size.*

*There are three gems upon this earth;*
*food, water and pleasing words.*
*Only fools consider pieces of rock jewels.*

*Oil poured on water,*
*a secret communicated to an unworthy person,*
*a gift given to a worthy recipient,*
*a sermon delivered to an intelligent listener:*
*these things, by virtue of their nature,*
*spread.*

*All creatures are pleased by loving words;*
*therefore we should spread them;*
*for of sweet speech*
*there is no problem of supply.*

*A man praised by others*
*is regarded as worthy,*
*whether or not he is.*
*A man praised by himself*
*is estimated lowly,*
*though he may be a god.*

*A crow can sit on a high place,*
*but he still is not an eagle.*

*Sinfully acquired wealth may remain for ten years;*
*but in the eleventh year it disappears*
*and takes everything with it.*

These thoughts from the *Nitishastra* suggest that he became a little more philosophical in his old age. But if the legends of his death are true, this may not be the case. Although no one really knows how the old mentor died, there is an interesting tale about his passing. The story goes that his old arch-rival Subandhu decided to get Chanakya into trouble. So he went to King Bindusara and revealed what only a small number of people in the older generation at the palace knew: that Chanakya had placed the poison in Chandragupta's meal that had killed Durdha, Bindusara's mother. The king was shocked, and made enquiries of his old retainers. He was horrified to discover that this was the truth: the old sage was responsible for his mother's death.

Chanakya, hearing that the young king was angry with him, decided that the time had come to end his life anyway, just as his former partner Chandragupta had done. So the sage gave away all his goods to the poor, and then went to sit on a dung-heap, determined to follow the Jains' example and starve himself to death.

But by this time, Bindusara had made further enquiries and got the full story—and learned how Chanakya had only been trying to make Chandragupta poison-proof. The king's old nurses, apparently, had told him the entire story of how Durdha had eaten her husband's dinner.

The king went to the heap of dry dung and rubbish, and tried to persuade the sage to return. But he would not. Bindusara stormed back to the palace and yelled at Subandhu to persuade Chandragupta to abandon his plan to kill himself. The sneaky arch-rival returned to the dung heap with a group of friends, and announced that they were going to perform a ceremony of respect for Chanakya. But while this was going on, Subandhu slipped a red hot coal into the dry heap of rubbish upon which the old man was sitting. The pile went up in flames, and Chanakya died as he had lived, a victim of sneaky, political intrigue.

Subandhu now had no competition for the role of palace wise man. But he produced no wisdom that has come down through the ages. As Chanakya would have commented: "A crow can sit on a high place, but he still is not an eagle."

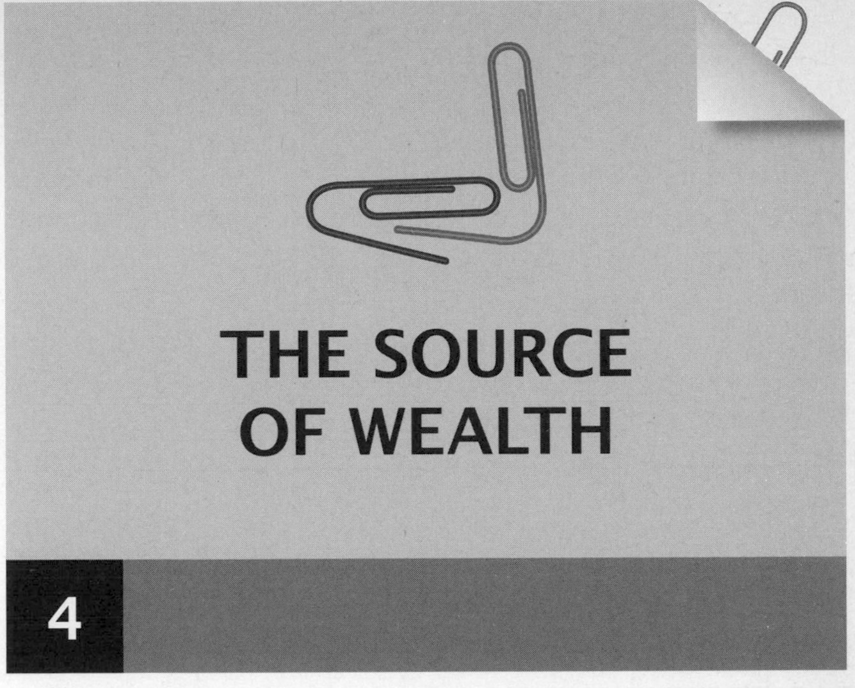

# 4 THE SOURCE OF WEALTH

**AT THE DAWN OF CIVILIZATION, A GROUP OF PEOPLE DISCOVER THAT CONCENTRATED ECONOMIC ACTIVITY GENERATES RICHES.**

## THE MOUND OF THE DEAD

IT WAS HERE. He could *feel* it. With a tug of the reins, Charles Masson stopped his horse outside the village, and cast his eyes at the hills around him. In many ways, it was an unremarkable scene. The land was undulating, with a steep slope to one side, and a gentler hillock to the other. The ground was dry, with the earth showing deep fissures, cracks that in places looked like the remains of earthquakes. Yet at the same time, there was a great deal of thick undergrowth in the folds of the valley, and stands of trees in the distance, some looking quite ancient. A number of the plants had thick, rubbery leaves, evidence of the extreme weather of this area: desert-like dryness in the summer, heavy rains and flooding in the winter, and stifling heat most of the year round.

The area was thinly settled in places, because of the harsh weather, and had been little explored by the Europeans who had surveyed much of the rest of the region. Yet it was an intriguing part of India, not least because of the exotic names to be found on maps of the area: Kadir Bet, The Salt Marshes, The Rann of Kutch.

Masson dismounted and walked his sweating, exhausted animal to an area of luxuriant grass west of the village where the other horses in the party were already grazing. The huge, over-arching sky was filled with a hostile glare as the traveler followed his guide, taking his ever-present notebook from his bag.

A few minutes' walk led them to an area in front of the small cluster of dwellings where the ruins were best viewed. Arriving at the spot, he surveyed the scene and started sketching. He saw the remains of what had obviously been a large castle, made of small, dark reddish bricks. You could see where the walls ran for a great distance in angular lines, and there were sections where the ruins still stood tall, although they were covered with vegetation. They were clearly very old, but exactly when were they built? Apparently, no one knew.

He noticed the age of the *pipal* trees on the site: although slow-growing, the trees in front of him were aged and withered. These trees could be many hundreds of years old, and it was said that some trees could live two thousand years or more. He wrote in his journal: "The walls and towers of the castle are remarkably high, though, from having been long deserted, they exhibit in some parts the ravages of time and decay. Between it [the castle] and our camp extended a deep trench, now overgrown with grasses and plants."

The topography of the land intrigued him. "Behind us was a large circular mound, or eminence, and to the west was an irregular rocky height, crowned with the remains of buildings, in fragments of walls, with niches, after the eastern manner."

Looking at the two hills in the area, it was abundantly clear to him that one was natural; the other was not. It was a curious, out-of-shape area of raised earth that must surely have held buried secrets. Although it was the mound that intrigued him, the main ruins were on the mountain-side. "The latter elevation was undoubtedly a natural object; the former being of earth only, was obviously an artificial one," he wrote. Who built it? And what for?

Masson was playing the role of an explorer; but that wasn't what had brought him to India. He was a deserter from the Bengal Artillery, a unit of Britain's East India Company. Headstrong and temperamental, he and a friend had stormed out of the regiment while it was stationed at Agra, home of the Taj Mahal. The pair had traveled to the west, and found themselves in the Indus River valley, an area not under British control.

Masson had not enjoyed his time with the British army in India, but he was fascinated by the country: its rawness and drama, and the feeling everywhere of undiscovered treasure, figurative and literal. He had the appetite for history that comes naturally to curious men, and after leaving the army, he had spent several years traveling across the land, learning about mysteries familiar to the locals but unknown to the wider world. He planned to write a book about them for publication back home, to make a little money.

From locals in the northwest region he had heard the legends of the lost world, a huge and highly advanced civilization that had existed in the Indus River valley, but which had been wiped out by the gods after the king of the place had taken up debauched and degenerate habits. It was a story of biblical grandeur, like the tale of Sodom and Gomorrah mixed with the legend of Atlantis.

Masson had arranged to join a party traveling through the area, with a view to uncovering treasures physical or intellectual. Now he had arrived, he tried to match what he could see in front of him with what he had heard from villagers. It wasn't easy to visualize exactly what the settlement may have looked like, but there was definitely something sizeable here.

He started writing again: "Tradition affirms the existence here of a city, so considerable that it extended to Chicha Watni, 13 *cosses* distant, and that it was destroyed by a particular visitation of Providence, brought down by the lust and crimes of the sovereign."

In the evening, when the temperature dropped, they decided to ride to the top of the strange, circular mound. Arriving at its peak, he was surprised at how large it was. "There was ample room on the summit to receive the party and horses belonging to it," he later wrote. From the top, he became convinced that below them was a great city from Indian legend.

The notes on Masson's visit to what we now call Harappa form only a small part of the book he eventually published as *Narrative of Various Journeys in Balochistan, Afghanistan and The Panjab* (London, Richard Bentley, 1842). Little attention was paid to these notes, and in the 1850s, the ancient bricks of the area were pulled up in their tens of thousands to be used as part of a railway built by the British.

But from time to time, several other historians and archeologists, English and Indian, took an interest in this region: it seemed particularly rich in legends, yet was almost totally unexamined. Many of them missed the treasures below the sand. In 1912, an Indian archaeologist called D.R. Bhandarkar went to a Harappa-like mound called Mohenjo-daro, the Mound of the Dead, and announced that it couldn't be ancient because "the bricks here found are of the modern type."

After all, no one in the ancient past could have made such things, could they?

It wasn't until 1921, after the ruins of Harappa had been disastrously looted for bricks by generations of builders that archaeologists became fully aware of the remarkable historical treasures buried in the mound, and in other mounds in the area. The more they dug into them, the more amazed they were at what they found. Under the earth was evidence of something that seemed totally impossible: in a stratum some *50 centuries old,* they found a large, planned city with a high level of technology. It really was like discovering Atlantis.

The confirmation in 1921 that a huge ancient city dubbed Harappa had been found was greeted with delight by historians. The ruins spoke of a civilization that seemed "too advanced" for its time; it meant that the history books would have to be re-written—something that historians, perversely, love to do.

Then, a year later, the truth about the Mound of the Dead was discovered. Mohenjo-daro was a city clearly built to similar plans and by people related to those who had built Harappa. The bricks were "of the modern type", but that didn't mean they were made recently; someone had built a modern-style brick factory churning out standardized items years before they should have been able to. What it meant was that the advanced city they had found at Harappa was no fluke: there was clearly some sort of nation here, a large, hitherto unknown civilization that had built a series of urban centers across a large swathe of land.

The findings not only excited archeologists, but also scientists, demographers and anthropologists. It is hard to express just how significant these discoveries were. For centuries, historians had assumed that the first human cities were the urban clusters of Mesopotamia, Egypt and China. Yet the Indus Valley ruins were of similar antiquity but were more astonishing for two reasons. First, their extent: the cities were in clusters, spread over an enormous area, dwarfing the other conurbations. The mounds were spread across an area larger than Western Europe. Second, the urban areas elsewhere in the world had grown organically: villages had blended into towns, towns had bled into each other, and eventually cities had been formed. But the Indus cities were different: they were partially or wholly planned, and carefully built on a grid system. This fact indicated that the people who erected them had a far higher level of societal sophistication than would be expected at such an early time in human history.

The historians had initially used the word "Harappa," the name of the first city found in the series of digs, for the ancient civilization, but then decided that it would be more accurate to use the term "Indus River Civilization." Yet over the next 80 years, as the size of the region became apparent, stretching far beyond the borders of the river valley, they have started to abandon the term and returned to using the term Harappan, using the name of the principle city for the civilization as a whole, following the example of Rome and the Roman empire. More recently, scholars think they have deduced the name of the place—but more about that later.

Astonishing discoveries are still being made in this region, much of which is still unexplored. But enough has been found to confirm that remarkably innovative individuals made their mark here, an extremely long time ago indeed.

But who were they, how did they work, and what can we learn from them?

While we are focusing mainly on ancient texts such as the *Arthashastra*, the *Bhagavad Gita* and the *Kama Sutra*, and the individuals associated with them, this particular chapter focuses on a community that produced writings that we cannot even read. Texts recovered from these sites have yet to be deciphered. Yet the level of innovation and strategic thought produced by the dwellers of this dusty and arid plain—made clear by artifacts, mysterious texts and archeological remains—is so remarkable that these unnamed geniuses deserve to be celebrated along with their more accessible, better-documented descendants. The people of this region are responsible for some of the most remarkable breakthroughs in human history—and provide valuable lessons for modern people in business.



## THE ANTHILL MAN'S IDEA

THEY THOUGHT HE was mad. And they were probably right.

Somebody—his name is lost to history—came up with an astonishing idea in the early bronze age, somewhere between 4,300 and 5,000 years ago. The notion was so strange that it is difficult to work out what sort of rationale he used to come up with such an idea. Of course, we know nothing about him, and we don't even know that he was male; although, given the inherent sexism of the earliest human societies—both hunter-gatherer communities and agricultural groups—it is likely that the major decision-maker in this instance was male.

His notion was this: let us build a super-village. Let us build a dwelling place not for one family, or one clan, but for a thousand people. Or forty thousand.

In those days, groups of humans had relatively recently moved from the primate model of existence, living in colonies off natural resources, to agricultural models, where people consciously selected plants, cleared fields and grew crops in large numbers. This move from one state to another was accompanied by a sudden and dramatic growth in the size of average human settlements. It was a major step in the development of modern humanity.

Those crop-based farming villages were always close to a major source of water, and tended to grow after a standard pattern. A farmer cleared a patch of land and planted one or more food crops. As his family grew and the families of others around him grew, the number of dwellings expanded from a few huts to a clan cluster of mud-and-timber shacks. Similar communities developed independently in exactly the same way in many places over the inhabited world.

But one man in the Indus River Valley had a different idea. He wanted to build a huge network of joined, interlocking structures that could house tens of thousands of people. The box-shaped dwellings would extend not just horizontally, but vertically. Some would be two, possibly even three-storey structures. When he sketched it out in the sand for his companions, it must have looked like nothing they'd seen before other than a gigantic, man-sized anthill of some sort.

The innovator was likely to have been a builder of some power, a respected, senior man who had moved from constructing homes himself to overseeing the construction of villages for whoever was the local ruler. But his companions must have thought that his time spent erecting homes under the hot sun had addled his brains. Why would anyone want to build a hut that extended for 5,000 paces or more in each direction? What would be the advantage? Surely it would be unbelievably impractical. It would take a long time just to walk to the fields. And how would you get to the water sources, if you were at the far end, away from the river? And what about sewage? No one would walk for an hour every time they had to urinate or defecate. The whole scheme must have seemed ludicrous, and the objections were surely legion.

Yet somehow the "super hut" man persisted in pushing his scheme, and managed to persuade people—probably one at a time—of the wisdom of at least trying out his plan.

And so the world's first planned city was put into construction. It was probably only the third city to appear on planet earth—the first two were in Mesopotamia and Egypt—but this urbanized cluster of city-dwellers was destined to grow far larger than either of those.

Picture our visionary but much-mocked Anthill Man standing in the brutal sunshine, supervising hundreds of workers as they built structures in ways that no one had ever tried before. This is the plan, he said, using a sharpened twig to scratch lines in the earth, and a long plank with marks on it to make sure the proportions all correspond with each other. "There will be an area here which will be Middle Town," he explained, scratching a large rectangle at the centre of the diagram. "Next to Middle Town will be a raised area that will be a palace, for our esteemed ruler to live in. And then, surrounding the center, will be a network of residences for the general population."

He then drew what we now call streets running north to south, across the entire map, and a number of narrower east-west lines too. The main streets were nine meters wide, and the side lanes were more like alleyways, either 1.5 or 3 meters wide.

This is not to say that he was building fresh on clear, open ground. There had been dwellings in Harappa for hundreds of years by the time the Anthill Man came upon the scene. But these were scattered, individual homes or conventional villages. His great contribution was to usher in a planned city and an age of obsessive standardization on a scale never before seen on this planet. By 2300 BCE, he was overseeing an operation that used standardized rulers, standardized weights and standardized designs for everything from bricks to plates to drinking vessels to city layouts.

He consulted a great many people, and perhaps not just architects and engineers. Some Indian scholars say they see signs that he spoke also to the early masters of *vaastushastra*, a type of geomantic art that is similar to the *feng shui* system of energy flow that was developed in China. (Others say that *vaastushastra* is a product of Hinduism and developed later.)

But before a single brick was laid, thousands of calculations must have been done as to how many bricks were needed—and what size each should be. Uniformity was all-important, and the dimensions of the bricks were agreed before work began. "All bricks will be one measure high, two measures deep and four measures long," the Anthill Man declared. Orders for millions of fired bricks measuring 1 x 2 x 4 were given to specialists, who must have spent years working at the furnaces to create the raw materials for the city. The bricks used were mostly heat-dried, as opposed to the cheaper, easier to-make sun-dried type, suggesting that there were enough resources, commitment and belief in the project to use the highest grade materials.

As the city took shape, its marvels must have become evident to the people who moved in. The city he built had a level of technology never seen before on this planet. No one had to walk to the fresh-water stream; there were man-made wells supplying drinking water at regular intervals. Nor did they have to use the distant fields for defecation (as many people in India still have to do today because of a general absence of public sanitation and amenities). Houses had their own latrines and bathrooms. There was a sophisticated drainage system, with sewerage tunnels that took waste out of town. He knew the value of recycling: the sewage was fed into the fields, where it became fertilizer for crops.

Streets were cut into the grid at angles that ensured that the wind would clear any garbage produced. Doors and windows were positioned in homes to bring light, air and perhaps *vaastushastra's* good fortune to dwellers. There were at least two main sizes of dwelling: large and airy ones for the noble families, and small ones for the common people. Streams were diverted to make useful pools of fresh water just outside the city walls.

The first city was clearly a success, because other urban centers were built on similar plans. There are elements of organic evolution in Harappa, showing that the buildings had to work around a series of dwellings that were already there. But this problem was partially solved at the next city, Mohenjo-daro, which is almost entirely planned, and completely solved at a third city, Dholavira, which appears to be entirely "built to order." Eventually, long after the original Anthill Man was dead, there was a string of modern cities that ran from what is modern-day Pakistan all the way to New Delhi.

The cities of Harappa, Mohenjo-daro, Dholavira and others were not just physically remarkable. They were places where organized civic governance was practiced, international trade took place and economics were studied. Further, the arts flourished, as clearly shown by the amount of artistic objects dug up from them. Numerous items of copper and bronze have been found. There was also pottery, and a large collection of terra-cotta toys. Then there are the famous seals of Harappa—which enabled residents to clinch deals by printing images of animals and pictographic script marks on to surfaces. This indicates a developed system of law. Indeed, some scholars believe a stone marked with symbols from this region is the earliest piece of writing in the world, dating back some 5,500 years ago.

As far as modern science is concerned, the archaeological investigation of this region is still in its infancy. There are thousands of square kilometers of land that have not yet been fully studied. Yet one key fact has been clearly established: a group of people in India, whose existence was barely known as recently as 100 years ago, must be listed as being among the very earliest pioneers of human civilization. It was this group who first produced planned, grid-based cities. They can be seen as the distant forefathers of modern planned cities such as New York.

And the truly amazing thing is this: the concentration of human energy in a small, tight space, generated wealth in multiple ways. Things changed hands at high speed, creating value. Money had not been invented, so a sort of "credit card" system was apparently developed, with families having a personal seal that could be used to mark their goods and authenticate transactions. It was small and square-ish and contained writing and a picture. (As time passed, the unicorn seal became the most common—perhaps the VISA or American Express of its time. "Unicorn? That will do nicely, sir.")

Furthermore, the burst of creative energy in that place appeared to have triggered an astonishing level of innovation in other fields. For example, it is believe that the first wheeled transport was developed by these individuals. It wasn't impressive by our standards, looking something like a bullock cart. But in that age, it was an astonishing piece of technology. There were probably a great many of them, and the community was proud of their transport: this is evidenced by the width of the lanes built for them, and the large number of toy carts modeled in clay that have been found. They may well have experienced the world's first traffic jams. This same community may have developed early technology that foreshadowed the invention of modern cotton-spinning operations, and must have been famed for the fine, cool, appealing textiles they produced.

Evidence of transactions "sealed" with their symbols showed that they traded far and wide, and had large numbers of dealings with Mesopotamia, the other main early civilization on this planet.

What did they call themselves, and who was their ruler? No one knows. Their written language has yet to be deciphered, and there are no records that indicate the names of their rulers or towns. However, there are a few tantalizing clues that apparently give us the name of their country. The Mesopotamians, whose written records historians have been able to decipher, tell us of a great trading community called "the Meluhhans," who lived in lake cities and used to dock their ships nearby and sell goods to them. The tell-tale seals of Harappa are found in Mesopotamia, and both places have goods that could only have been imported from the other.

The people who settled in India in the following centuries called themselves the Aryans ("the nobles") and referred to the folk who lived there earlier as "mlechhas," a word that came to be used as a term of contempt, as colonizers might talk of "primitive natives." That word was not made up of phonemes in the Aryans' own speech, suggesting that it was an attempt to pronounce a local word. "Mlechha" is similar enough to "Meluhha" to provide a possible element of confirmation.

So the great trading nation in the desert, with its huge multiple cities spread over a vast area, was probably known as "The Meluhhan Land of Water Cities" or something similar. The people were proud and successful. But they could not have known at the time that factors outside their control meant that their miracle cities were doomed.

## ON INNOVATION

LOOKING BACK FROM our vantage point 4,300 years later, the Meluhhans seem like early miracle-workers, the builders of a genuine Atlantis, an early pocket of human genius. In reality, though, they are unlikely to have been any different from any group of individuals who tries something new. The innovators who led their community to try a series of untested ways of town-construction must have suffered the same ups and downs, the same series of rejections and successes, the same one-step-forward-one-step-back progress that anyone building a large, untried structure experiences. Yet they persevered, and achieved something that made human history. And not least, they left us with some remarkable lessons.

***Trust your local neighborhood genius: true innovators are hard to come by.***

It's a truism in business that genuine innovation is far less common than one thinks. While one naturally tends to think of entrepreneurs as people who do something new, in fact the vast majority of business people do something old, but do it a little differently. For 99% of commercial organizations, the road to riches is to build a slightly better mousetrap, not invent a revolutionary new form of rodent-capture device (although the advertising will say the opposite). How many times have you seen automobile advertising that says something along the lines of: "It's not a car. It's an invention." This is stylish advertising, but it's wrong. It is a car: a metallic box with a wheel at each corner.

True innovation is hard to come by. But it does exist. It tends to flourish in situations where there's a lot of human energy. That's not to say that someone in slums cannot come up with a brainwave. But for practical purposes, the Silicon Valley model is more common: a group of people, be they Meluhhans or dotcom geeks, will gather in a single place and the sparks thrown off by their activity and interaction will ignite a host of creative ideas.

Killer ideas do pop up from nowhere from time to time—almost everyone has them occasionally. There will be times in your life where you, or one of your associates, will come up with an idea that is genuinely revolutionary, although whether it will ever be more than just a notion is up to a number of other factors. Perhaps this new idea of yours will change the rules of the game, and will have analysts using phrases like "paradigm shift." If you are very fortunate, you or one of your teammates will be a highly creative individual who will have fresh, original ideas on a regular basis. And occasionally, one or other will work.

True creativity is a wonderful thing—and a rather rare one. We still know relatively little about it. It is an ability that some people have to connect ideas in their brains in new ways. There are always tiny "sparks" traveling along the ganglions of the gray matter, or running across the *corpus callosum*, the bridge that connects the left and right halves of the brain. One day, one of these bits of bio-electrical energy jumps across a divide in a direction it had not tried before, notions in your head are combined in new ways, and—hey presto—a brilliant idea is born.

Should an entrepreneurial person grab the ball and run with all the bright ideas that people in the team have? Probably not. The nature of business means that only one in a hundred or one in a thousand is going to change the world in any measurable way. But a number of very successful modern companies—Pixar, the animation firm, is a case in point—have a culture where they encourage all employees to be innovative, and they work hard to keep ideas flowing and growing, however off-beat or left-field they are. They know that true innovation is a rare resource: if you see it sprouting anywhere in your organization, take action to feed and water it. It could pay enormous dividends in the long run.

But be prepared for failure. Even the best ideas sometimes fail—ideas that have "success" written all over them. Consider the mini-disk: a tiny, re-writable audio CD that was marketed in the 1980s under the belief that (a) people would like to the ability to record their own CDs, in the same way that people in the 1970s recorded tape cassettes, and (b) that people would enjoy having small, portable media. Both ideas were bang on target, and demonstrably true. By the year 2000, people *were* recording their own CDs in the millions, and by 2005, small and attractive portable digital devices *were* the happening thing. But the mini-disk, by then, was consigned to a small place in digital gadget history. It became clear that it had offered people the future before they were ready for it.

A slightly different but equally tragic story, in business terms, was the development of the Newton by Apple Computers Inc. Innovators at Apple believed that the public would buy a handheld computer that you could write on with a special pen. It would contain a notepad and a diary and be a sort of personal digital assistant. Huge sums went into the development of the Newton, but it was mocked because of imperfections in the handwriting analysis function. The product failed, but the idea was spot on. Ten years later, handheld devices with improved handwriting functions were selling in the millions, although not from Apple.

Getting a bright idea is step one, but that first step is a relatively small one. Making the idea work commercially is step two, and it is a giant leap.

***Your team does not have to conquer the world by itself: it just has to produce a world-class business model that other people can use elsewhere.***

We talked earlier about the importance of building a team. The world has reached a level of complexity where it is almost impossible to achieve anything significant working alone. Even the loneliest jobs of all cannot be done in isolation. Perhaps your skill is producing masterful illustrations with a 2B pencil and watercolor paintbrush. While it is unlikely that anyone can help you create the illustration, you still need a network of people to turn your skill into a commercial career: at the very least, you need suppliers of raw materials at wholesale prices, you need an agent to market your work, a gallery owner to publicize it, and you need publishers to buy it and take it to the general public.

These days, you would probably also need a friend or partner who was familiar with computer software and hardware, as these have become key factors in the production and marketing of images. Even an artist needs his team; everyone does.

The Anthill Man had an idea. It was probably something that started in the mind of a single person, or perhaps a couple of individuals who saw how human energy was different when people were clustered together. But to make this idea into a physical reality for thousands of families must have taken an enormous number of individuals. The magic of team-building is happening all around us, from small scale to huge scale.

When two people get married, they create something bigger than a pairing of individuals: they create a new structure, a legal, psychological, emotional entity that becomes the basis of a new family. As I said earlier, the total is always bigger than the sum of its parts when it comes to human beings. Think how much more true that is when the organization you build is not one or two or three people, but one or two or three thousand people. The Anthill Man found this out with his city of 40,000 people.

Many of us have big ambitions. We want to be successful business people. We want to create goods or services that are used by thousands, or tens of thousands, or even millions of people. Yet we baulk at the necessary steps we have to take to make those dreams into realities: we don't have the courage to build a big team to realize our big ambitions. Well, here's the news: you don't have to conquer the world. Just build a model that other people can use.

The Anthill Man put together a team big enough to build a single city. This inspired the building of similar cities nearby, who used the same plan. We now know there are scores of sites where the Meluhhans built towns and cities, and it is unlikely that the original Anthill Man was personally involved with any but his own. Yet the eventual result was a sophisticated nation that was huge, covering a large swathe of Pakistan, India and Afghanistan. Indeed, one of the Meluhhan sites is in a place called Shortughai, which is in the part of Afghanistan that borders Russia. The franchise was highly portable. It was a discovery that more recent innovators have also used. Ray Kroc did not build more than 30,000 branches of McDonald's. He built a model that could be replicated around the world by franchisees. Howard Schultz did not fit out the 11,700 branches of Starbucks around the world, nor did he use the same sort of franchise system that Kroc used. Instead, he bought out existing coffee shop chains, or used local partners to acquire local knowledge and local property, and employed vast teams of managers around the world to replicate the original Seattle branch.

When you are putting together your business plan, there's an exercise you need to do. It won't come naturally, and it will cause you some pain, but it is important to do it anyway. It's this: cut yourself out. Rewrite the business plan so that it will work without you. It doesn't matter if you are the chief cookie-baker, or the chief illustrator, or the main inventor, or the only teacher in a one-person school. Turn the business plan into a structure that works without you; with a hired hand filling your space. This will have two effects. It will remove the disastrous over-emphasis on the talents of a single individual that most entrepreneurial business plans have. And it will make the plan portable, so that if it succeeds, it can be replicated elsewhere. This does not necessarily mean that someone else will replicate it. It just means that it has a structure that will work independently of you, if you should one day want it to.

One more example: A starving poet wants to commercialize his skill. Selling books of poems is not going to make him rich, or even enable him to feed his cat. So he sets up a class where people come to listen to him talk about poetry. He is inspiring, and has a way with words, so his class is a success. The business plan works, but it can only ever be small: a single poetry class taught by a single, inspiring teacher. But imagine he did it differently. He writes down all his lectures to make them portable. He makes data files of the examples he uses to illustrate his points. In each class he teaches, he spots one or more people who also have a way with words. These people become his lieutenants or assistants in subsequent courses. Eventually, they are teaching some of the courses independently, representing him and paid a small fee by him. Once the team is in place, they start other creative courses, teaching people how to write songs, screenplays and short stories. Eventually our poet is the dean of a college of literary arts, and actually teaches only when he feels like it. Now he is rich and successful and has the time and money to devote himself to what he likes to do best: writing poetry. Only this time, neither he nor his cat has to starve.

***Go for the niche that nobody else wants, and then use the advantage that uniqueness gives you.***

Now here's a risk that might be worth taking. Estate agents always tell us that the three most important issues in real estate are location, location and location. You have to be where the action is, they say. But they are wrong. This is a simplification, and simplifications are necessarily misleading. The property agent's mantra may be a useful general one to follow for the home-buyer. But for the strategic business person, we have to consider the issues much more carefully, and we know that hunting for opportunities is the key to success. General platitudes are of no use to us. Choosing a location is a decision that includes trade-offs—and that means hidden pitfalls and disguised opportunities. Yes, a good location is a wonderful thing to have; it's nice for a hundred reasons to have your office right in the center of town. You enjoy the prestige, you feel the convenience of being close to the amenities, transport links are great, and your staff are happy. They have a wide choice of restaurants at lunch time, and can do a little shopping on their way home. Putting location first is the safe choice.

But you pay a premium to be in the heart of town. What is that premium, exactly? Are you paying 50% more than you would be paying if you moved to a less fashionable area? Or is it 100%? In Hong Kong or Tokyo or New York, it may be 300%. How do these sums factor in to the rest of your operation? What size is the advantage you would get by choosing an off-center location? Would the benefit be small, medium, large, or sensational?

Too many businesses never consider this question. But the Meluhhans did. They took the risk of choosing a location that was well away from other tribes, and gave them lots of open space in which to build. The area they chose was arid, but there were streams and rivers running through it, and they were smart enough to know that streams can be diverted, channeled and controlled. They knew that there was a wet season, when the rivers rose. By taking action to control the water supply, they took large swathes of unwanted land and turned them into an area they could use. They started with dry ground, and finished with cities famed for their water features: this was truly a miracle for their age.

Now of course the question of taking the niches that other people do not want is not just a physical one. I used the example above of finding a good site for your office. But I want you to take this concept metaphorically as well.

Imagine that you are starting a language school in Beijing. You already know that the most popular language that people in China want to learn is English. You discover that there are thousands of English tutorial colleges in the capital of China. You could set up your own and try to do it better. Or you could try something else. An idea strikes you: why not set up a school to teach

Spanish? Like English, Spanish is one of the biggest languages in the world; and yet it is a less obvious service to provide. As the world continues to shrink, and people travel more and more, it is going to be clear that a number of Chinese speakers, just like English speakers, will find the need to learn Spanish.

In China, just as in India, you find that business operates on what I call the "no small numbers principle." In most communities around the world, tiny niches exist for people who want to provide very specialized services; to set up such a service, one needs to calculate whether there is going to be enough business to make it worthwhile. But in countries where the population is large, there are eventually going to be enough bodies to fill almost every niche. Think how true this is of countries that contain a billion people, such as China and India. Even if you are providing a service in which 99.9% of people have no interest, the 0.1% left over adds up to a million customers: that's because there are no small numbers in China or India. There will certainly be more than enough to fill your school of Spanish.

***Build a little magic into every bricks-and-mortar structure.***

Although we know little about the culture of the Meluhhans, there are possible indications that they followed geomantic principles in the way they built their homes. *Vaastushastra*, like *feng shui*, is a mixture of practical home-building tips, mysticism and superstition. To people five millennia ago, it seemed only natural to include a little invisible magic in the plans for homes and workplaces. As these geomantic skills become popular again today, our modern society is only now starting to relearn important things about the man-made environment that have been forgotten for thousands of years.

The next time you open an office, don't just think about the numbers of chairs, desks and power sockets you need. Build a little magic into the structure as well. You could employ a *vaastu* reader or a *feng shui* master. Or if that's too esoteric for you, choose your own flavor of magic: build into the plans a folly, or an *objet d'art*, or a prayer room, or a play room, or a space in which to meditate. Buildings need to be more than bricks and mortar. Your financial officer will complain, but ignore him. Your staff will like it, your visitors will be impressed and your company will stand out from the crowd.

***There is no physical resource as likely to generate wealth as human flesh and blood.***

Think of something portable that's worth a lot. What do you think of? Gold and silver? Computers? Designer suitcases? Jeweled necklaces? We think of commodities we can pack into boxes and sell, probably. But it doesn't take many years of experience in the business world for one to discover the truth: people are the key to generating wealth. They are the *only* key. It's the flow and concentration of humanity that make a business. Your fish restaurant is not really about the lobsters in the tanks. It's about the non-piscine creatures who walk in through the front door, enjoy a meal, and then go and tell their friends and relations. This is no less true in the gems and precious metals industry. Everyone in it knows that there is something of the emperor's new clothes syndrome in their sector. A tiny glassy rock is just a tiny glassy rock; 100% of the value in that business is in its customers' eyes. The rocks take their value from the people who value them. This is even truer of the bottled water industry, which inspires people to pay for a substance that is usually provided free in their homes.

Meluhha was a large, thriving society because it was a mass of creative humanity—indeed, one of the first of its kind on the planet—not because of any physical resource that existed in the main cities, which were built in a hot, dry land. The number of bodies crammed into a single community had interesting repercussions that triggered changes in society: some of the larger dwellings and spaces were almost definitely schools, trading rooms, lecture theatres, bazaars and sports grounds. We know for a fact that some of the cities had swimming pools. The project, once it reached critical mass, would have taken on a life of its own. And as business thrived, agricultural and other surpluses would have been generated, which enabled the city to expand. This leads us to a related principle:

***Taking unorthodox steps will create unorthodox opportunities.***

With their planned cities and standardized weights and measures, the Meluhhans clearly found that they had created new jobs. When homes fell down, they had to be built the same way: there must have been specialist artisans who maintained the buildings. There must have been surveyors who stopped people remodeling their homes in ways that interrupted the streets or blocked the alleyways—in other words, compliance officers from some sort of planning department. There must have been water experts who made sure the water systems flowed properly. There must have been draftsmen who mapped out the city, and who took the plans (or sold them) to the people who built other urban centers in the area. There must have been a huge factory churning out bricks, and that would have meant laborers, foremen, quality control supervisors, raw materials buyers, accountants and so on.

There is physical evidence that the environment was unpredictable: several of the cities suffered floods, and were later rebuilt on the same plans. So there must have been librarians, or information specialists, who stored the maps and plans and took them out again when needed. The floods must have been devastating; and I cannot help but hope that the original Anthill Man did not live to see his creation destroyed by the rising waters of the nearby rivers—or that he lived long enough to see them rebuilt. Harappa was flooded and rebuilt several dozen times.

Yet the cities did not survive until modern times, and there is a reason for that. In the short, medium and long term (by which I mean for years, decades and scores of years), the cities of the Harappan plains thrived. But in the ultra-long term (by which I mean centuries and millennia), they did not. And the reason they disappeared can be summed up by another principle:

***Underneath the business cycles that power activity, there are other cycles, bigger than you could ever imagine.***

## LOST CITIES

WHAT HAPPENED TO the cities in the desert? Why did they disappear? Did they flee or were they invaded? Why were they emptied before the earth closed over them, forming the mounds of the dead?

Archaeologists have grappled with these questions since the cities were discovered in the 1920s. At first, it was thought that invaders from the north, a tough tribe of nomadic, horse-riding people known as the Aryans, poured into the area and devastated the Meluhhan cities. That theory is being challenged by some unorthodox historians with Hindu nationalist sympathies. They claim there is a gap between the periods during which each of the peoples dominated the area. Furthermore, if newcomers chased the original inhabitants away, why did they not take over the sites? The cities were not invader-occupied, but abandoned, an important difference.

Today, there's a growing belief that a number of factors, but principally the environment, turned the Meluhhans out of their homes. Clues come from more recent digs. Several hundred kilometers to the southeast of the two best-known cities, Harappa and Mohenjo-daro, a similar planned city called Dholavira has been found. It is of similar antiquity, taking shape some 5,000 years ago. At 50 hectares, it is large, although considerably smaller than the biggest of the three, the 250-hectare super-city of Mohenjo-daro. And again, despite its position in a dry area, it was filled with water features. It has been estimated that a third of the land of Dholavira was used for collecting and storing water. Excavated only over the past 20 years or so, it provides pointers as to what may have ended the Harappan civilization.

If you take a stroll around Dholavira, you find that it fits into a neat parallelogram, just like the others. It has a "city square": an area of open land in the heart of town that stretched nearly 300 meters long, and was probably used for public assemblies. The cities were founded on their ability to control water. Dholavira was planted on a slope between two streams, one of which was diverted to flood a reservoir at the city wall. Although the flow of the streams changed with the seasons, the use of a system of reservoirs meant that the city had a year-round supply of fresh water. It has strong city walls, some five meters thick at its base. Interestingly, the upper-class part of town has its own fortified walls, as if the rich started to feel that security might be an issue and wanted their own mini-walled city. Class must have become an issue.

Some scholars have noticed that war in Mesopotamia coincided with the decline of the Meluhhans, suggesting that trade routes were severely disrupted, cutting the income of the people of the dry plains. This theory probably has some truth to it. These lake cities in the dry plains were very much founded on international trade. It was business that kept them buzzing. A major disruption in trade routes and business activity would have caused problems for cities that were rather delicately constructed, which were "on the edge" literally and metaphorically.

But while trade problems were probably a troublesome factor, most scholars think it was likely to be the land that finally defeated them. The substrata show signs of several severe floods, and possibly earthquakes too. Some of the rivers and streams in the area probably dried up and disappeared. I can picture the crowds gathering in the City Square at Dholavira and receiving the bad news from the engineers. An earthquake had diverted one of the streams, and drought had dried up the other. The reservoirs would be empty within days. People would have to leave the city or the rulers would have to find some way to bring in water, until things returned to normal.

Over the decades and centuries, these problems gradually mounted, in much the way that our understanding of global warming has crept into general consciousness today. It must have been difficult for them. Suffering periods of extreme dryness, interspersed with floods, the delicate systems of the water cities must have been damaged and repaired several times—and then, the environment would eventually have wrecked them beyond repair. There are signs that the cities were eventually abandoned, and then later re-occupied, and then abandoned again. It must have been difficult to leave a rich, technologically advanced city that had stood for hundreds of years, but the underlying environmental cycles of drought and flood, stretched over centuries, were eventually enough to drive away the hardiest inhabitants. (The lesson for us today, in these times of strange weather, warming temperatures and melting glaciers, is clear.)

Underlying fears turned to a realization that things were changing on a major scale. They probably felt that they had angered the gods, or some sort of great, divine bull. (Given the preponderance of bull images, they probably worshipped some sort of divine cow, which puts them in line with the beliefs elsewhere in India.) Perhaps it was the decadent behavior of the rich, or the ruler, or the priests, or the people who lived in the "posh" walled-off part of town. They fled for their lives, moving to friendlier climes and intermarrying with other tribes, and the earth closed over the great cities of the dry plains. The communities continued to exist for an extremely long time—not centuries, but millennia—as legends in the consciousness of the people of the region, and were still talked about hundreds of generations later, when the Anthill Man's bricks, perfectly designed and manufactured, were dug up to be re-used.

But the biggest compliment of all is the fact that studies are taking place to learn from the water-supply systems in Dholavira. Modern water-engineers in India say that in dry parts of the country, today's systems work less well than those put together by the people who built the world's first planned cities, at the dawn of recorded history. Anthill Man, rest in peace. You did your job well and today, more than 40 centuries later, modern man is trying to learn from you.

# 5 ON WINNING AND LOSING

**MINUTES BEFORE HE HAS TO KILL OR BE KILLED, A SOLDIER CONFRONTS THE GREAT QUESTIONS OF LIFE. HIS SEARCH FOR ANSWERS IS PRESERVED IN THE *BHAGAVAD GITA*.**

## A PRINCE HESITATES

A MILLENNIUM BEFORE the birth of Christ, a personal crisis occurred that has resonated through the ages. The time: circa the year 950 BCE. The scene: a battle, straight out of *The Lord of the Rings*. Imagine a huge field, with two ferocious armies facing each other. The soldiers were wearing a variety of shapes of body armor and were carrying heavy-bladed swords, or light, fast-flying spears, and most had thick shields of wood, bronze and other materials. Behind them were phalanxes of archers.

The participants in the battle were not just human. Or at any rate, the fighters involved believed that among them on both sides were creatures who were non-human, or who were super-human. The gods were involved in this war, too. The combat, it was clear, was going to be extremely violent. The field would shortly be drenched in blood. There were also large numbers of mounted cavalry and armored elephants.

The combatants were driven by clashing allegiances. One army was an occupying power, lead by a brilliant general under the command of a blind but charismatic old man named Dhritarashtra. The commander of the forces was a man known as General Bhishma, known as the Grandfather, despite the fact that he had taken a vow of celibacy and had no children. He was leading the battle on behalf of the larger army, the Kauravas.

The smaller, opposing army was led by two younger men, challengers who were fired by a determination to return the deposed, rightful king to his seat. They were brothers. The younger one's name was Arjuna, and he was traveling by chariot to his dangerous position near the front of his army. He was the lead archer. Commanding the force was his brother Yudhishthira, who stood in the center of the front line. They were the Pandavas.

The prize was the throne of Hastinapura, the center of the region now known as Haryana. It had originally belonged to the Pandavas' side of the family, but Yudhishthira, the oldest son of the Pandavas, had lost his kingdom to his cousins, the Kauravas, in a game of dice. Choosing the honorable option, they had fulfilled their pledge by withdrawing from the kingdom for 14 years. But that time had passed, and the Pandavas were returning from exile in the forest lands to reclaim their kingdom.

But their cousins had decided that they liked ruling a large kingdom, and had decided to fight to keep it. "We will not return a piece of land as big as the tip of needle," a member of the occupying family had said.

And so the war had become inevitable. Most feared was the Kauravas' commander Bhishma. The man's original name was Devavrata, but he was called Bhishma, which meant "he of the terrible oath," after an exceptional vow he had taken. It was a bizarre story: his royal father fell in love with a woman whose family was deeply ambitious. The parents of the woman said they would hand over their daughter to him only if their family would become uncontested heirs to the throne. To enable this to happen, the king's son Devavrata generously took a life-or-death vow to stay celibate all his days. He was known as Bhishma thereafter and his popularity and fame soared. He was considered the honorary patriarch of both sides of the war-torn family, the Pandavas and the Kauravas.

The fear and excitement must have been palpable in the steaming summer air at Kurukshetra, "the field of the Kurus." Arjuna's chariot was being pulled by powerful horses and would have been moving fast. The vehicle was controlled by a charioteer who whipped and steered the horses, while the passenger, propped against an internal ledge inside the body of the vehicle, handled the weapons.

As co-commander of the Pandavas' army, Arjuna would probably have been giving his equipment a final check before the fighting commenced. He was the third in a line of five brothers in the family, but had aged a great deal in the past months. It had been a suffocatingly tense, difficult period, when repeated attempts to obtain a diplomatic solution were rebuffed. He was a peaceful man by nature, and must have found the rising tension in the community almost unbearable. And now the time had come for bloodshed. The Pandavas had assembled a small but powerful fighting force.

But as the horse-drawn vehicle comes in plain sight of the front ranks of the occupying force, Arjuna shouts to his driver to pull the reins and slow the horses. The driver turns to look at his leader.

"Stop," says Arjuna. "Stop here for a while." The chariot comes to a halt, as do the chariots of the soldiers following directly behind him. Why has he stopped? I can imagine the senior men behind him reining in their horses, suddenly anxious.

What a moment that must have been. I'm sure Arjuna, with the battle of his life ahead of him, had never felt so alive—and yet he had probably never felt so dead. Every inch of his body would have been flooded with adrenalin as he prepared to fight to the death; in such situations, one feels as if one is almost walking on air. Yet at the same time, given his personality, I think he would have felt unbearably heavy, as if his limbs were made of metal. What was causing this heartache? Was it fear? Was it cowardice? Was it the thought that many of his men would inevitably lose their lives?

No. It was none of those things. It was sadness—for his enemy, and for his community. There was nothing so tragic, he realized, as a civil war, a fight among brothers.

Men, certainly in those days, were built for fighting. Human beings clustered in groups of tribal peoples, and it was rare for anyone's lifetime to come and go without a member of their family having to fight to the death at least once against some group of invaders—or alternatively, for them to be drafted as invaders to take over another tribe's lands. There was nothing unnatural about fighting and killing; indeed, for men of that era, lethal combat was a normal part of life.

But civil war—ah, that was not the same. And it was consideration of that all-important difference that had caused Arjuna to stop his chariot. Civil war meant killing members of your family. It meant killing your friends. It meant a community, a tribe, a family turning on itself.

At this distance, he could barely see the faces under the helmets of opposing forces. But he didn't need to. He knew exactly who they were. During the previous months of unrest as tension mounted and as his political moves to regain power were repeatedly rejected, it became clear who was on whose side. Some of his friends, family members and associates had joined him. Others had been drafted to defend the occupier. They had no choice in the matter. Lined up against him there would be cousins he grew up with, his playmates and acquaintances he had known from the old royal court, also teachers who had lovingly schooled him. Many of his friends would be lined up with their spears, ready to kill him. And so would many strangers; just ordinary people of the city who had been living peaceful lives before the fight started, and who had done the only thing they could do: when drafted to take up arms to defend their city, they had done as they had been told. Their reward would be to be hacked to death by him and his men.

How could this be right? In a flash, Arjuna realized that human society disastrously tended to engineer situations where some people would be winners, while others, inevitably, would be losers; losers who would have to give up everything, including their lives. As he hesitated at the edge of the battlefield, he became acutely aware of the humanity and brotherhood of all individuals. And it was this feeling that drew him to do something that a great leader would never normally do: he asked his chariot driver for advice.

"Driver," Arjuna says. "Tell me, in the name of God, what are we doing?"

The question may have been rhetorical, but the reply wasn't; for asking the driver for advice turned out to be exactly the right thing to do. For the charioteer was no ordinary man. He was Lord Krishna, the story goes. And the conversation that Arjuna and his magical driver had on the edge of the battlefield has become a classic of discursive literature, in the same way as has *The Book of Job*, another volume in which an unusual situation triggers a lengthy and analytical discussion of the human condition.

## BE DRIVEN BY PRINCIPLES

TODAY, IN THE 21st century, we understand perfectly what Arjuna had realized. It is something that the literature of strategy, management and business has re-discovered in recent years. It is the principle that groups of human beings, left to their own devices, will set up brutal win-lose battles between themselves, and blood will flow—in war, red blood on the battlefield; in business, red ink on the bottom line. Gain for one is loss for another. Life is a zero sum game. You can't win unless someone else loses.

But does it always need to be this way? And if not, in what situation does it not need to be this way?

Arjuna was asking these questions thousands of years before any writer of popular business manuals came up with the phrase "win-win" situation, but the points he was making remain valid today. When there are winners, must there also be losers? When is fighting wrong, and when is it right?

The driver in this story was said to be Krishna, and his counsel was filled with otherworldly wisdom. He made a number of points in poetic language that stretch over many chapters of the story of Arjuna's battle, a long poem known as the *Bhagavad Gita*.

How should we interpret this? Clearly the *Bhagavad Gita* is not to be interpreted as a work of journalism. It is a poetic recreation, probably written about the fourth century BCE, of an incident that is believed to have happened up to a thousand years earlier. I have not demythologized this story, because it is generally accepted for what it is: not history, but an imaginative poem based on historical events and real people. Furthermore, it is part of the great Indian scripture known as the *Mahabharata*, but does not have the "feel" of the rest of it. Most scholars believe it is a later insertion. Technically, it is considered a *smriti* text, which is a secondary rank of ancient writings. Yet the value of the advice in the story is so great that it has achieved the status of *shruti*, or the highest, most divine grade of "revealed knowledge." Indeed, the *Gita* has become one of the great religious scriptures of all time.

As Mohandas K. Gandhi, the Mahatma, said, "The *Gita* is the universal mother. I find a solace in the *Bhagavad Gita* that I miss even in the Sermon on the Mount. When disappointment stares me in the face and all alone I see not one ray of light, I go back to the *Bhagavad Gita*. I find a verse here and a verse there, and I immediately begin to smile in the midst of overwhelming tragedies—and my life has been full of external tragedies. And if they have left no visible or indelible scar on me, I owe it all to the teaching of *Bhagavad Gita*."

So what did the soldier learn on the battlefield? The first thing Krishna tells Arjuna is that he should not over-emphasize the importance of death. Death is not what is important, but life, and how it is lived. And this action, this war, was all to do with living life the right way, by taking righteous action. It was how one lives, not one's death, that is a person's central focus.

To fully realize this, Krishna continued, you have to learn to live life in an enlightened manner. You must let go of your small self and follow the principles of the great consciousness. Only if you detach yourself can you transcend the attachment to the material world, and only then do you have a chance of becoming part of what is infinite. He tells Arjuna that he is worrying because he is thinking about the deaths that will follow the war. But what he should be thinking about is the importance of doing the right thing. And in this case, to fight for what he believes is right, even though it will mean pain or death, is the correct thing to do.

There will always be a discord between the confusion generated by the human senses and the serene intuition that a person can pick up by being in tune with cosmic unity, Krishna explains. This is why self-control is so important. The root of discord, and other forms of human suffering, is the agitation caused by desire, the primary motivator. One should instead douse the flame of desire, by stilling the mind. Become disciplined and detached and then one can be assured of having the right focus—and making the right decision.

He anticipates the thinking of the New Testament's Paul of Tarsus, by explaining that acts of goodness are not what are needed to win salvation. Rather, the human being should take a different route and fully surrender to the absolute, and thus have his sins forgiven. The man speaking with the voice of God says: "Setting aside all virtuous deeds [*dharma*], just surrender completely to my will. I shall liberate you from all sins." This does not mean that you should not do virtuous deeds. The *Bhagavad Gita*, like all other texts featured in this book, emphasize their importance in everyone's life. But you should not rely on virtuous deeds to win salvation. That comes only from surrender of the self to God, or the absolute principle.

He urged the soldier to be aware of the importance of doing one's duty in life with no thought of reward. If there is something you have to do because it is the right thing to do, then that alone should be reason enough to do it. There should be no thoughts of personal gain, or indeed with any consideration of the consequences. A man who makes every sword-stroke count, whether he is fighting or rehearsing for a skirmish, will perform as best as he can. But if he focuses on the end goals (Will he win the battle? What if he loses the tournament? What is the prize, anyway? Is it worth it?), he becomes emotional and distracted. His standards slip, and so does his sword.

"Your motivation to take a particular action should be in the action itself, not to the fruits of the action," the charioteer says. Krishna calls upon Arjuna to abandon attachment to winning or losing, because only then can he achieve true evenness of mind, and the power that genuine detachment brings with it. He tells the soldier to be wary of emotions: "From attachment springs desire, and from desire comes anger, from anger arises bewilderment, from bewilderment loss of memory, from loss of memory, the destruction of knowledge, and from the destruction of knowledge—you die."

Arjuna listens patiently to the messages that were coming through, and then he realizes the key principle that should be driving him in this difficult situation: *Your business is with the present deed, not with its result*. He realizes that he should not be end-focused, nor should he be dealing with the question of whether the end justified the means. No; for the means were justified or not *in themselve*s. If the action he was taking was the only righteous way to react in this situation, then there were no choices. He must do what is right. Absolute principles are higher than anything, even blood, even family loyalty, even death. In peacetime, it is wrong to kill. In times of war, sometimes to kill is the only right thing to do.

Arjuna made his decision. He would fight.

But just before he raised his sword and screamed for his men to charge into battle, he saw a movement on his left. The most senior man on his side, his older brother Yudhisthira, was walking forward by himself. And he was removing his armor.

## LESSONS FROM THE *GITA*

YOU HAVE TO HAVE nerves of steel to be in business today. Business commentator Charles Abbott said: "To manage a business successfully requires as much courage as that possessed by the soldier who goes to war." He felt that the corporate soldier, just like a military peacekeeper, eventually brought about a positive result from which, ideally, everyone should benefit.

But let's look at the lessons we can derive from the *Gita*:

***The only way to achieve a complex victory on multiple fronts is to focus purely on the present step at the present time; for life is no more or less than a series of nows.***

When we see the achievements of others, we see only the results. We see J.K. Rowling at the top of the bestsellers' list. We see Madonna at the top of the music charts. We see Ray Kroc's McDonald's restaurants spreading around the world. It is only natural for us to see the achievements of people around us and to think: *I could have done that*. After all, we all have a bit of creative commercial flair, and many of us have a lot of the stuff. These stars stare out at us from celebrity magazines and we think: I could write a children's book. I could compose a song. I could set up a restaurant. That could have been me.

It's true: you could probably have done any of these things, given the time and energy and will power. But so could a dozen, a hundred, a thousand, a million other people. The act of creation that produces a product or a service is important, but it is not by any means the sole element that makes things happen, that alters the course of our lives, that changes the world. There are many other factors that come into play. When we are trying to achieve a level of success in our business or personal lives, the number of things to think about is legion. Where does one start?

We start by focusing on the now, and the deed we are doing at this moment, the *Gita* says. Paul McCartney and John Lennon were writing songs in the ultra-creative early 1960s, when almost every street in Britain would have contained at least one house where young people with guitars or pianos were singing their hearts out. But Lennon and McCartney were more focused than the other kids; they performed night after night at clubs in Liverpool and in Hamburg, and had been working for two years before they had their first international hit. Were they planning to become the most celebrated popular musicians in the world? No. They were simply doing their jobs, gig by gig: singing and playing and earning a buck. But while they were doing that, they were also developing their voices and song-writing talents for their stardom to come. Yet that was merely incidental. They were focused on the *now*. They spent their daylight hours writing song-lists and practicing numbers for the particular gig they were doing that night. When they played the concert that caught the attention of a record producer, they didn't even know he was in the audience.

The same can be said for our other examples. Joanne Rowling was not trying to create a phenomenon that would shake up the world of books and movies. She was trying to write a good story that someone would publish; that was all. Penniless and burdened with the responsibilities of being a single mother, it was hard work. And when she had finished it, she had to sell it to a publisher or agent—which was even harder work. Again, while we are bombarded with news and statistics about her success, how many millions of copies she sold, and how much money she has made, we too easily forget that her book was rejected, not once, but several times. At any point in the fight she could have given up, decided it was too hard, and tucked the manuscript onto a shelf where it would have been forgotten and the moths would have had it for supper. But she didn't. At both the key stages in the creation of the phenomenon, she focused on the now. Her job at stage one was to write the story she had in her head. Her job at stage two was to get the story she had written taken up by a reputable agent or publisher. The events that followed could not have been predicted at that time—and a good thing, too. Had she had some sort of vision that her stories would make her one of the richest people in the world, she would have probably thought she was going crazy.

Similarly, Colonel Sanders was not focused on turning Kentucky Fried Chicken into one of the most popular restaurant chains in the world. He just wanted to get the latest franchise worked out—and the next, and the next.

Like Arjuna, we all have battles ahead of us. If you are in business, you have a product or service to sell. You have a market to grab. You have targets to achieve. You have efficiencies to implement. But human nature being what it is, we set our eyes on that far-away target and start walking blindly toward it. We are like a marathon runner who sees nothing but the finishing line—but not the potholes on the road, the obstacles around us, the competitors in the way, the untied shoelace below us; any of these things, on their own, can prevent us reaching our goal. Don't live in the future—that's the message of the *Bhagavad Gita*. If you do, you will be distracted and anxious. The good marathon runner instead focuses on taking each step at the right time. He knows that a single misstep can cause him to sprain his ankle and put him out of the race. He knows that he needs to concentrate on taking each step correctly—and that's all. A marathon is a long race that can be broken down to perhaps 40,000 steps, each of which has to be taken correctly. Focus only on the future target and you may or may not perform the correct individual actions to get you there; focus instead on taking each step properly, one at a time, while watching the road directly ahead of you, and breathing in rhythm, and you will find that as you take the 40,000th step you will have made it to your goal.

***Absolute principles must be treated as such. Falter on these and the ground will forever shift below your feet.***

Arjuna was a man with a mission. He was fired up with the task that the gods and his community had called him to do. He had to gather an army and overthrow an occupying force. He had to get the rightful king, his elder brother, back onto the throne. He had to win a war. His mission was clear. Indeed, he had been focused on nothing else but this task for months. Deep down in his heart, he knew what he was doing was right.

And yet now that he came down to it, there was a succession of grossly discomforting aspects to his task. It was a civil war; he hated the thought of breaking up with his own cousins, of fighting with them, of killing them. He knew that war was the most terrible thing that could happen to human communities: for it to happen to his own friends and family was unthinkable. And he personally knew many of the people in the other side, whose combatants included his former teachers, including one he particularly loved.

At the last moment, he wanted to know if the horror could be avoided. Death was a terrible thing. So should we not call off the battle, find another way? This would have been a good and noble sentiment: except for the fact that they had tried the other route and failed. Injustice was prevailing, and someone had to stop it: that task had fallen to Arjuna, and he had to complete his mission.

Arjuna's dilemma is something that we can all identify with. Sometimes we face situations where all alternatives seem bad—we feel trapped; we feel there is no clear road ahead; we want to turn around and run and hide instead.

But that's never the right thing to do. His situation reminds me of a saying attributed to Martin Luther: Sin bravely. You have to do things wholeheartedly. Most of the time, you know what wrong and right are; they are usually perfectly clear and distinct. But occasionally, you get into situations where the choices and outcomes are unclear. Sometimes you are stuck in a place where all your choices seem bad. In those situations, we are tempted to dither, to vacillate and to do nothing at all. No, says Martin Luther: *Sin bravely*. Make your choice and move on.

The charioteer makes a similar argument in the *Bhagavad Gita*. If you have to choose between different actions, you do what needs to be done: you make the choice and get on with it. What you should not do is select inaction. We've all worked with people who, when faced with tough business decisions, simply defer them, in the hopes that an answer will present itself later. But business is not like that. Introducing an uncomfortable hiatus at a moment that needs decisive action doesn't take you closer to your goal; it either freezes you to the spot or moves you backwards. It is well said that the cruelest form of refusal is delay. If you approach someone with a business decision to be made, he or she needs to say *yes* or *no*. But very often today, the response is no response: you are merely told that a decision has not been made, but will be made in due course.

I recall working with a charitable organization who suspected that its sponsor, a major bank, was going to withdraw its support. The sponsorship money failed to arrive in the charity's coffers on time. When enquiries were made, the workers were told that there was no problem, and they should be patient. For months they were quiet, and it was only toward the end of the financial year that the bank executives worked up the courage to tell the charity that they would not be sponsoring them after all this year. The bankers were probably motivated by good intentions. It was hard to deliver bad news; so let's delay it, and see if something happens; perhaps the bank's charitable arm will change its mind; perhaps some other cash will turn up; besides, we are so busy at the moment; we should really focus on other things; who knows what will happen in the long run? But what actually happened was that the delay ate up the time period that the charity needed to find a new sponsor. A *no* delivered politely in good time would have been far kinder than the alternative the bankers chose. It would have sent the fund raisers back on the road with their bowls. They could have had a long period in which to find a replacement sponsor, and the project would have been fine. In practice, the delay turned out to be the cruelest form of refusal: they ended up with no cash from their sponsor, and a very short time indeed to find a new sponsor. In that instance, they succeeded in finding one, but everyone involved learned a hard lesson: it's kinder to say *no* than to say *later*.

***The end never justifies the means.***

The charioteer lectures Arjuna on the ethical questions in the battle. The soldier is worried about whether the end justifies the means. Is the goal worth it, if it means that a battle must be fought and people of our community must die? Krishna argues that doing the right thing is more important than anything, even blood connections. There are absolute values that must be treated as such.

Today, we see corporations violate the laws of natural justice all the time. They know only legal statutes. And they employ full-time staff to find ways to get around the ordinances, despite the fact that laws are there to protect people, to stop individuals or the community from being hurt. These executives know, or care, nothing about natural justice—yet it is one of the deepest strands of being in the human soul. These days, people are hostile to phrases like "absolute values." They associate such strong ideas of right and wrong with religion, with dogma, with a lack of tolerance. But in fact the concept of "absolute values" runs far deeper than dogma. The religious did not invent it. It is a natural part of our make-up.

Anyone who spends time with children will know that at regular intervals, one child will have an argument with another and will storm up to the adult taking care of them, their eyes blazing with fury, and utter the words: "It's not fair." Knowing what is fair and what is not is something that comes naturally, and it comes from the deepest part of our beings. Children don't need to consult lawyers: as they become aware of themselves and the people around them, they naturally develop a powerful sense of fair play. They know what is right and what is wrong. It is one of the most valuable and important building blocks in the make-up of our personalities.

Somewhere on the road to adulthood, many of us lose this. And when we join corporations, we can move dramatically in the opposite direction. It's one of the most terrifying things about modern society that many businesses employ accountants and tax specialists solely for the purposes of finding loopholes in the law. They won't express it like that in polite company, but they know it's true. Rather than run the business justly, people run their businesses along the very outermost edges of the limits prescribed by law: they make sure they give the absolute minimum; they go as far as they can over the line; and then they employ lawyers who look for loopholes that they can use to step safely over it. If they go too far and get caught, they don't apologize. They issue a statement pointing out that while they will pay compensation in this instance, they do not admit to any liability.

When most businesses were family businesses, the laws of natural justice ruled. If your food supplies came from a mom-and-pop store on the corner, neither the customer nor the vendor would do a thing that would violate the rights of the other; how could you, since you would have to live in close proximity to each other for the rest of your lives?

But now, things are different. Products and services are provided by faceless corporations to customers they never see. And because of this, the ethics of business have changed. The overriding question that business people ask themselves today is: What can I get away with? Motivated by their allegiance to their shareholders instead of their customers, they are not interested in value or fair play. This departure from the laws of natural justice to the "values" created by legal maneuvering is one of the most tragic developments in modern society. Justice and the law grew up as twin brothers. Today, they are not only estranged, but they are too often arch enemies, working against each other.

In contrast, we can look at business people such as J.R.D. Tata, who ran the Tata group of industries in India for many years. He was famous for his ethical standards. It cost a lot in lost deals to refuse to bribe politicians, and it cost a great deal of hard cash to restrict his firm to never use the black market. Yet the ultimate result was that Tata became trusted internationally, and ended up as one of the best-known global brand names from India.

## GOING INTO BATTLE

WE'RE BACK ON the plain of Kuru. The war is about to start. The Kaurava army stands in the east, and the Pandava army in the west. Hundreds of thousands of individuals stand prepared to die.

But as Arjuna and the other troops look on, they see Yudhishthira, eldest son of the Pandavas clan, marching forward. Is he starting the fight by himself? No, he is dropping his weapons as he walks. He leaves his sword and spear and shield on the ground, undoing his helmet as he moves. His men must have been shocked.

On the other side of the field, the Kaurava forces would have been bristling to start the battle, but they were surely caught offside by this unexpected development. They watched him discarding his chest plates. How could they throw a spear at this unarmed man, walking alone toward them?

Yudhishthira was one of the most memorable flawed heroes of India's past. It was he who had rolled the dice and gambled away everything—his possessions, his kingdom and even his wife Draupadi. In the popular story, he and his family had been utterly humiliated when his opponent, a relation named Shakuni, had tried to take possession of her immediately, by trying to strip her clothes off in the gaming room, in front of everyone. Wise, fair-minded Bhishma the Celibate, the Grandfather, was one of several people who protested at such a terrible event. And the old blind elder Dhritarashtra had agreed that such incidents could only cause great harm to the people. He ordered that Yudhishthira's losses be cancelled.

But Shakuni had spotted that Yudhisthira was an addicted gambler. He offered him one last throw of the dice, offering him the chance to win back everything he had lost and more—or be exiled from his own kingdom for 14 years. The player had been unable to resist, and had gambled away everything. The Kauravas had taken over the city of Hastinapura, with Dhritarashtra on the throne. And they were not giving it up.

But now the battle for supremacy was about to start—and what was Yudhishthira doing? He walks steadily and calmly across the gap between the two armies, and does not slow down as he reaches the front line of Kaurava warriors. It was clearly an act of courage to approach the enemy unarmed, and the soldiers instinctively part to let him through. The Kaurava army had 10 divisions, with ranks of soldiers in front, elephants behind, cavalry on both sides, and the leaders at the back. Clearly, the co-commander of the Pandava forces wanted to speak to the leadership of the enemy force. Was this a form of surrender or one last bid at averting the war by diplomacy?

It turns out to be neither. General Bhishma signals for his men to allow the unarmed Yudhishthira to approach him. The younger man reaches the old patriarch and drops to his knees. He bows his head low. "Grand sire," he says. "I am your child. I cannot go into battle without a blessing from you."

Bhishma smiles. "Then you shall have it," he replies. The old man calls down an invocation for Yudhishthira's destiny to be fulfilled. There is silence on the battlefield except for the call of the Grandfather to the heavens.

Afterwards, the co-commander of the Pandavas' army rises to his feet and quietly returns, unmolested, to his side of the battlefield. He picks up his armor, sword and shield, puts it on—and gives the battle cry.

The war starts.

The battle raged for 18 days, with massive losses on either side, although probably not the "millions" that the old stories claim. There were many poignant moments, as family members and acquaintances clashed.

One of the most memorable was the death of Bhishma, beloved of both sides. It was on the tenth day of the fighting. The Kauravas, under the able leadership of Bhishma, had had the upper hand at the beginning of the battle, but the Pandavas had recovered, and the battle was balanced—with both sides losing men at a steady rate. Casualties mounted fast, and it was heartbreaking to watch.

Arjuna became desperate to stop the battle and decided that the only way to do that would be to kill Bhishma, the old man he loved. He felt that the loss of the patriarch, tragic though it would be, would dishearten the enemy to such an extent that the Pandavas could get the upper hand and win the day. He hit upon an unusual plan. Bhishma had a strange relationship with one of Arjuna's soldiers, a man named Shikhandi. The old man had got it into his head that Shikhandi was the reincarnation of a woman who had cursed him and died. (Bhishma had defeated the woman's suitor in battle. The bested man had then given her up to the old warrior, but being celibate, he had not wanted her; as a rejected woman, no other man had, either.) Arjuna decided to send Shikhandi to confront Bhishma, curious to see how the old man would react.

As day broke over the bloody field (both armies had agreed that there would be no fighting between sunset and sunrise), Shikhandi was dispatched in the direction of Bhishma's chariot, with Arjuna following close behind. Recognizing Shikhandi approaching, Bhishma lowered his bow. He refused to shoot at him. To the old general, Shikhandi was a woman, albeit one reincarnated as a male, and it was expressly forbidden in the law to use any weapon against a female.

Making the most of the old man's confusion, Shikhandi and Arjuna pumped Bhishma's body full of arrows. It is said that the old general fell forward, but he did not touch the ground, instead being suspended off the floor by the number of arrows embedded in the front of his body.

The Pandavas' next target was Drona, a powerful warrior who was responsible for the deaths of scores of their soldiers. He was a strong man with only one weakness—he had an overpowering love for his son, Ashwathama, who was also fighting in the battle.

"Tell Drona that his son is dead—and he will be so disoriented that we can overpower him easily," one of the Pandava brothers told his oldest brother Yudhishthira.

"But I cannot tell a lie," came the reply. Yudhishthira, in atonement for his sins, had pledged never to speak a lie—a vow that was almost as famous on both sides as old Bhishma's vow of celibacy had been.

"I know," said the younger brother—who then produced an elephant named Ashwathama, whom he stabbed in the heart. The elephant fell to its knees and then rolled over, dying. "Ashwathama is dead," he said.

In the next engagement, the brother, whose name was Bhima, shouted out to Drona that his son was dead. Drona knew the Pandava fighters' wily ways and refused to believe him. He turned and shouted to Yudhishthira: "Is this the truth? Is my son dead?" Drona knew that Yudhishthira could only speak the truth.

He replied carefully: "Ashwathama is dead. He's dead." Unable to mislead anyone, Yudhishthira added in a quiet voice: "Ashwathama... *the elephant*."

Drona was momentarily confused and lowered his sword—and the Pandavas took the opportunity to kill him.

At the end of the 18-day war, the Pandavas triumphed, but with heavy losses on both sides. Neither Arjuna nor Yudhishthira celebrated their victory. Both had lost their sons. It seemed that Arjuna's fears had been correct: the destruction of so many family members was devastating.

But the winners had to claim their prize, and marched on the city. Yudhishthira was crowned king of Hastinapura in addition to Indraprastha, the city the Pandavas had built in exile.

And what did he do? Yudhisthira decided to give the job of king of Hastinapura immediately back to the man he had taken it from: and so the throne was returned to old blind Dhritarashtra. What Yudhishthira had really wanted, he said, was to reclaim his family's honor, and by winning the battle he had done so. The battle was not about land and not about power: it was about principle.

A wild horse was released to wander freely for a year. Arjuna and a troop of soldiers followed it, under a ceremony that decreed that the wild horse running free would establish the boundaries of the kingdom.

As the months went by, a time of peace and plenty returned to India, and Arjuna saw at last that the tragic war had been necessary.

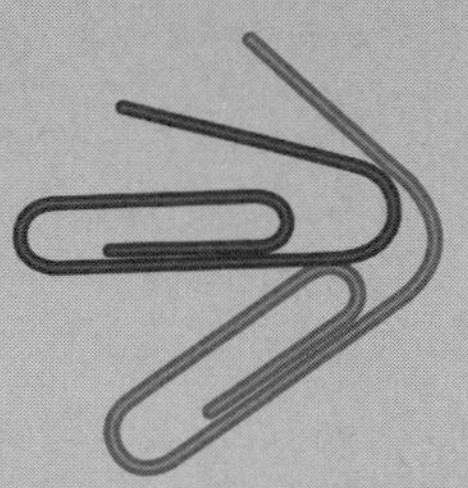

# THE GOAL IS NOT WHERE YOU THINK IT IS

6

**SIDDHARTHA GAUTAMA EXPERIENCES GREAT WEALTH AND EXTREME AUSTERITY AND DECIDES THAT BOTH ARE FALSE GODS. HE DISCOVERS THAT TRUE FULFILLMENT LIES ELSEWHERE.**

## THIS BOY'S LIFE

THE NURSE SNEEZED. The boy screamed and ran away. I can picture them, tearing down the corridors of the building, the child in a panic, and the nurse even more frantic. Given his importance, she would probably not have been allowed to use his personal name. But carers and their charges inevitably generate their own private language, and one imagines she must have shouted after him using a succession of nicknames or endearments.

Mansion homes of the time would probably have had rough-hewn flagstones, and running would always have been a little risky: misjudge a step by half a centimeter, and your foot catches the edge of a paving slab, causing you to lose your center of balance and tumble flat on your face. I don't know how many times he stumbled, or she stumbled, or if she finally caught up with him, or whether he outran her. But whatever happened, she must eventually have managed to find him and ask him what had frightened him. Deep down, I suspect she already knew.

The story of Siddhartha Gautama, a boy born to the leader of the Sakya clan in Kapilavastu, a place now situated on the Indo-Nepal border, is one of the best-known tales we will examine in this book. Yet at the same time, it is one of the hardest to tell. In keeping with the rest of this volume, we will look at his tale dispassionately (a word he would have loved), and take a historian's stance when analyzing the legends. It's a big job involving heavy use of the red pencil. His story has been told thousands of times over, in children's books, in religious books, in cartoons and even on the Hollywood screen, in movies such as *Little Buddha*. But the historian cannot retell it without disinterring it from the layer upon layer of embellishments laid upon its surface. This exercise is difficult, but it is supremely worth doing. Underneath the fairytale version of Siddhartha's life is a compelling story of a real flesh and blood human being who achieved something remarkable and communicated it to the world. One cannot help but be inspired by the tale of a privileged man who set aside his wealth to ask questions and came to conclusions that put him into the top rank of the most influential human beings who ever lived.

Another reason to look again at this oft-told tale is to set the record straight: his story, as well as being embellished, is usually simplified to such an extent that it becomes misleading. In the West, certainly, he is traditionally seen as the ultimate ascetic, portrayed sitting with his eyes closed under a tree, his only possession being a loin-cloth. Yet he was no ascetic; indeed, he rejected the life of asceticism as firmly as he rejected the life of luxury. But let us not jump ahead. We need to go right back to the beginning.

There are enough sources and traditions that enable us to identify, with a reasonable degree of certainty, some key facts about the life of the man who was to become known, in Sanskrit, as the Awakened. His birth date was the full moon of the sixth lunar month: his disciples recorded that much for us. There is much scholarly dispute about the year of his birth. Traditionally, it has been taken to have occurred about 500 BCE, but more recent scholarship sets the date a little earlier, at about 450 BCE.

His father was a man named Shuddhodana, leader of a nation-clan known as the Sakya, which was on the borders of a more powerful state called Kosala. In the fairy tales, he was born a prince in a palace in a great kingdom. But in truth, Kapilavastu was never a great city. It was a town, and its ruler was elected. So Shuddhodana can be seen more as a mayor or local general than a king. He was of the warrior caste. Siddhartha's mother is accepted by all sources to have died at birth or shortly afterwards. But the ruler had a number of wives, and the motherless child did not lack maternal affection. He was raised by a stepmother named Mayadevi, or Mahaprajapati, who was said to be related to his mother (possibly her sister).

The event that gave shape to Siddhartha's life and enabled him to discover truths that would influence human thought occurred early in his life and was entirely outside his control. It was a clash of ideas between his father and a visionary by the name of Asita. As one would expect, the holy man, asked to speak during the baby's birth celebrations, made a grand prediction that the new son would grow up to be a great man. But what does it mean to be a great man? Asita, for reasons known only to himself, said that Siddhartha would be great in one of two ways:

he would be a great leader or a great holy man. The implication was that the two could not go together.

The statement is said to have caused great concern to Shuddhodana. The child might grow up to be a holy man? Holy men in India were respected but they were not powerful. The phrase "holy man" was most often associated with monks and wandering ascetics known as *sadhus*; people who had no possessions, and in the eyes of some, often questionable levels of sanity. There was and still is a general belief, and not just in India, that mystical genius and irrational madness are divided by only the thinnest of lines. In much of the world, this notion is merely matter of idle discussion, but in India, the results can be seen in many places. Emaciated *sadhus*, wandering on the edge of society dressed in ash, trinkets and little else, appear to be mentally deranged: yet their derangement is often seen as the factor that gives their statements and prophecies value.

Shuddhodana took the prediction seriously, we learn. He interpreted it as a threat, or at the very least a grave warning. He made up his mind that he would take control of the child's destiny: the boy would grow up a leader; under no circumstances could he be allowed to grow up a holy man. The ruler drew up a strict series of household regulations that were designed to protect his new baby against the "horror" that might befall him. The child must be sheltered from anything that would allow him to think about the big questions of life; about the existence of God or the gods; about suffering or death; about prayer or ritual; about morality or ethics. Instead, the child was to be spared the emotional pressure that comes from trying to deal with these issues by being kept ignorant of them; he would grow up as a commander of men from the moment of his birth. Wealth and power, privilege and luxury: these were to be the only things he knew.

Whether this actually happened in the way the legends claim cannot be proved. The biography of the founder of Buddhism is not derived from a set of books like the Christian gospels, which are full of names and dates, and appear to be written by people who were present at the events, or who may have at least interviewed eyewitnesses. Ashvagosha's book was written at least half a millennium after Siddhartha's birth, and very likely depended on stories passed down through generations. That in itself doesn't make them automatically unauthentic. However, he used his very lyrical and poetic imagination, describing the child as a divine being who could stroll around and sermonize within minutes of his birth. "The Himalayas shook and lotuses fell out of a cloudless sky" as the walking, talking baby strolled around. It's a good read, but unfortunately turns Siddhartha into a poetry-spouting divine cipher. Instead, there is much historical evidence that he was a real, flesh-and-blood human being who grew to become an adult driven by a passionate desire to find non-materialistic fulfillment. This suggests that at least the Asita part of the story was true. The motivation for his search must surely have been the fact that he was denied the chance to examine these issues in his childhood.

## THE MEANING OF PROTECTION

AND SO WE SEE Siddhartha living a privileged existence. What would it have been like? How did this thick layer of protection form the child's personality? It's hard to hear the story without wondering how a child living in material comfort, with all his wants and desires instantly supplied, could have grown up to be so moralistic, thoughtful, and anti-materialistic as he did. In other situations in which people have grown up wealthy, with all their whims fulfilled, they suffer from personal problems—think of the Roman Emperor Caligula, for example, or even the eccentric singer Michael Jackson. It has been wisely said that you should be careful of what you ask for, because you just might get it. So how come little Siddhartha, the ultimate protected child, did not grow up a hedonistic monster?

Perhaps, to some extent, he did. Or perhaps it is all a little more complex than that. When one examines Shuddhodana's edict more closely, and considers the practical difficulties of following it, the answer to that question starts to come into focus. The father's edict could not have been followed in any serious way without setting off a series of repercussions; repercussions that undoubtedly would have had a dramatic, or even traumatic, effect on a child's life.

The child, by decree, was never allowed to encounter sickness. What that would have meant was that any associate of his who became ill in any way—a servant who caught an ailment of any kind, for example—would have to have been whisked away, never to be seen again. Relatives who deteriorated in some manner, who became frail or disabled, would have been removed from the mansion-home instantly. Childhood associates who were damaged or blemished—perhaps a classmate who lost a finger in an accident, or broke his leg—would disappear, never to be seen again. And if someone whom Siddhartha loved, like his personal nurse, for example, should happen to sneeze—would the child not be terrified that she would disappear, as all the other people who suffered sickness had vanished?

Children's minds are in some ways more sensitive than adults'. So perhaps the attempts to put Shuddhodana's edict into practice would not have generated a Caligula-like monster, but a confused, insecure little boy who received endless material possessions he did not need, but constantly lost, in the most baffling circumstances, exactly the things he did need: carers, friends and relatives.

Then there was the issue of his mother, who died at or soon after his birth. Since the child was not allowed to know anything about death, what was he told about his mother? He surely must have wondered why other children were doted upon by their mothers, but he had no mother, nor was he able to find out why she was no longer with him. Mahaprajapati may have looked after him lovingly, but there's no reason to believe that she pretended to be his mother, rather than his aunt.

Furthermore, consider the aspect of Shuddhodana's edict that he must not see the suffering outside the walls of the house. While he may well have lived in the most luxurious home in the Sakya nation, nevertheless, these were not sophisticated times. The palaces of the TV and movie versions of his life are inventions. Kapilavastu was not a grand city. It was just a town, and possibly little more than a staging post between the bigger cities of India and what is now Nepal. The ruler's house would be what we see as a relatively humble building—and unpleasant for Siddhartha, if its doors really were locked to keep him in. To be prevented from leaving home under any circumstances would surely have had an effect on the boy. However large his garden, he must surely have wondered about the world outside—and living on the borders of the high country of Nepal, it was almost inevitable that there would be glorious distant mountain tops seeming to hang in the sky. What must the child have thought, when everyone else was allowed to go in and out of the home, and he was stuck inside, year in and year out? A palace can be a prison. It is not the presence of bars that makes a prison, but the absence of freedom.

He is said to have lived well into adulthood under a highly sheltered, protected system, the traditions say, and was married at the age of 16 to a princess called Yashodhara, soon after to become a father. It was not until he reached his late 20s, that things began to change.

It appears logical to me that it was precisely because he was never allowed to ask the big questions of life that they became his obsession. But however it happened, everything changed when he was 29. That was when he left home. In the fairy tale version, he rides out into the town for the first time and sees four shocking things that give rise to questions within him. I have no problem accepting that he eventually left home and discovered much to shock him in the world outside. But you don't have to be a psychologist to realize that in doing so, he would have suffered a degree of trauma. People who do not leave a building for many years tend to develop a condition known as agoraphobia. Although this is often erroneously explained as fear of open spaces, it is really a condition in which an individual has had so little experience of being in unfamiliar situations that he suffers uncontrollable episodes of terror upon leaving the enclosure in which he has been staying.

If he had really been cooped up for most or all of his life, leaving home must have been horrific, considering what he found outside. Think about the sights that this ultra-sheltered man saw: people who were poor, sick, suffering and dying. The town, like any other, would have contained individuals suffering from a variety of ailments—some were probably missing limbs, while others may have had parts of their bodies eaten away by some pathogen or other. The poor must have been present in large numbers, living in misery on the streets. There would have been broken-hearted people, wailing over the deaths of their parents or children. He would have seen corpses, waiting to be burned or buried. And there would have been the ascetics, with their skeletal bodies and mad eyes.

Rather than riding out into the throng, a look of noble concern on his face, as in the Hollywood version, it's hard to imagine him having any other reaction than racing back to safety, and fervently thanking his father for protecting him from the horrors of life. I see a terrified, agoraphobic Siddhartha trying to block out the horrors he had seen, and returning to his comfortable, pain-free, materialistic ways of life within the warrior-chief's walls. Thanking his father for locking him in the house, the young man would surely have reburied himself in the trappings of wealth.

But you can't put a genie back into a bottle, you can't unscramble an egg, and you can't unsee something that you have seen. Once Siddhartha knew that people outside his safe little world lived lives of suffering, sickness and death, he would not have been able to get their pain out of his mind. Especially considering that he was being groomed to be a warrior leader in the mold of his father. Furthermore, this discovery would surely have linked up to those distressing episodes he must have had as a child, in which people he loved who became sick would simply disappear.

And then there was the mystery of his mother to be solved: something horrible along these lines must have happened to her—illness, suffering, death.

Most people reading this book are likely to be familiar with the concept often known as "middle-class guilt." We have food to eat and shelter over our heads; but we feel guilty that many people do not. Siddhartha must surely have felt the same thing, but on a much larger scale, and perceived more violently. We struggle with it in small stages as we grow up and learn about the sadness in the world around us. But Siddhartha, because of his father's edict, went abruptly from one reality to the other. He was not given the chance to develop the ability to cope with the existence of suffering. Others gradually become aware of pain and inequity in the world and find a way to do something about it: some of us devote our spare time to supporting charities, or helping to run soup kitchens, or become politicized and campaign to help the less well off. In contrast, Siddhartha was faced with a much starker choice: he felt he had to choose between staying in the protected life of luxury that his family had arranged for him, or joining the real world of pain and suffering.

He chose to make a renunciation of his life of wealth. He turned away from the temptation to retreat forever back into his comfort zone, enticing though that option must have been. Instead, he emerged from his shell and abandoned everything he had known. He was determined to resolve the different aspects of life and to find answers to questions that he had never known existed. Perhaps he realized that only if he found the answers for himself, could he help others. Or perhaps his motivation was largely selfish, based on his need to resolve contradictions that were tearing him apart.

I won't go into all his adventures and discoveries, although I do recommend that anyone who is remotely interested in his life take time to read about this remarkable man. We know from various records that he journeyed to the big cities, the bright lights of his day and age: these were cities such as Sravasti, Vaisali and Rajagriha, the royal compound of the Magadha region. At the last of these, he met the king. This was before the days of the Nandas and the Mauryas, and the palace was occupied by a man named Bimbisara. The king apparently urged Siddhartha to go back and take up the life indicated by his caste: he was supposed to be a *kshatriya*, a warrior. The king even offered to help set him up with whatever he needed. Did he need some money? Some soldiers? Siddhartha politely declined. Clearly the king had misunderstood him. He was looking for something else.

He was looking for answers, but before that, he was looking for a question.

But what was it? What did he really need? The answer eventually came into focus. Destiny had so shaped the life of Siddhartha of the Sakya Clan, son of Shuddhodana, that the most important question humanity has to face came into clear focus in front of him: *How should a man live?*

Siddhartha, at the age of 29, left the palace of the king of Magadha and wandered into the world with nothing in his hands but that question. Since material possessions and family had led him to no answers, but had merely obscured the question, he threw them both off.

The first place he looked for answers was with the ascetics: the monks. *How should a man live?* To be rich and wallow in a life of luxury was not the way a person should live. There must be another way. Perhaps monks had the answer: they were the most obvious examples of people who did not respect money and comfortable homes. First, he traveled to the northeastern territories and joined a monastery, where he signed up for training in the ascetic life. He joined a group of other religious men and did what they did: they rose at the crack of dawn, lived simply, begged for alms and practiced various techniques of self-deprivation. He lived in the humblest of accommodations, and survived on the plainest of food. Famously, onions and garlic were forbidden, because they made the food tasty.

He did this for months. But that life did not lead him to satisfaction. Siddhartha felt that this was a step in the right direction, but it did not feel like the whole answer: there was no feeling of transcendence; there was no magic; there was no indication that this was how a man should live. With the sensation-hungry drive of the young, he and a small group of companions decided that it must be because the monk-teachers were relatively old and soft; and so perhaps they were failing to be hard enough on themselves.

So they parted from the others and wrote themselves a manifesto in which they deprived themselves of worldly goods, places to sleep, food to eat and water to drink in a far harsher manner. They became the most austere of ascetics. It was a hard life—and dangerous, too. Living with absolutely nothing, Siddhartha entered another stage of his trials—and came close to starving himself to death. Having eaten and drunk nothing for days, he found himself in pain and hallucinating. He was barely hanging on to life when he saw that death in itself was not the answer. He lifted his skin-and-bone body, and made a big decision. He accepted food from a woman named Sujata.

The shock of nearly slipping away to an early grave made him realize that this route, too, was wrong. How could dying be seen as an answer to the question of how a man should live? It could not. It was the opposite of an answer. Death would merely be an acknowledgement that there was no answer to the question.

Wandering through the cool, magical forests of northeastern India, he sat and tried to collect his thoughts. He remembered an instance in his childhood when he was watching his father in the garden. It was spring. The sun was bright. Shuddhodana was working with his men, starting to plough the field. Siddhartha remembered sitting under a rose-apple tree. All around him was the smell of freshly turned soil. On his skin was the warmth of the sunshine after the winter. He recalled how he had drifted into a state of bliss; how he had become one with the moment; how he had been released from every emotion, every thought, every craving, and how he had felt he was, for a few seconds, a human being who was in exactly the right place and the right time and the right state: an integral part of the universe. That state: that was the answer. That was what he had to find again.

Siddhartha abandoned asceticism—to the dismay of some of his companions, who thought he was being weak-willed and defeatist—and looked for another way. He sat under *a bodhi* tree and started to meditate. A passing goat-herder offered him some buttermilk. He accepted. Self-deprivation, he decided, was wrong in itself. Under that tree, he sat for days—and came into a state of being that he later referred to as enlightenment. By extreme focusing on the now, he developed a system of transcendence. In this state, it became clear to him that indulgence and self-mortification were two extremes, both of which were the wrong answer to the question as to how a man should live. The middle path was the right way.

He felt different from that moment on, and referred to this time as the moment of awakening.



## THE AWAKENED

THE LIFE OF SIDDHARTHA of the Sakya Clan is filled with lessons for us: lessons that can be applied to all parts of our lives, from the toughest of our business battles to the most personal parts of our inner lives. It is hard to find a figure in history who encapsulated the mystery of the human condition as dramatically as he did. He changed the way people think—and people who learn about him even today need to go through the same thought processes that he and his supporters did.

***The goal is not what you think it is.***

We all have goals, and most of us think we know what they are. We want to be happy. We want to be comfortable. We want to be loved. We want to feel satisfied with our achievements. We want to have enough money to indulge ourselves from time to time. We want financial security for ourselves, and for our children or family members. We want to be appreciated. As we get older, we find we want to be remembered. We want to leave our mark on the world. In moments of lucidity, we can sit and think of the things we want, and most of us can make a fairly long list.

But if we step back and examine the minutiae of our lives, we discover something else: we spend almost no time pursuing the things that we claim are our major goals, our important, long-term, life-shaping goals. Instead, we devote almost all of our energy following the short-term, relatively trivial goals that society sets for us. We become controlled by things that are petty but urgent. Did you finish that report? Pay that bill? Send that invoice? Sign that document? Revise that paper? Send off that letter? Read that newspaper? And the next day, we do all the same trivial things again, and the next, and the next.

And on the rare occasions we managed to set aside time to concentrate on bigger goals, we find that we choose those that are almost uniquely from one sector—the financial achievement area. The targets set by our communities are to do with becoming high achievers, and that means being big earners. We are all encouraged from our school days onward to get "good" jobs, so we can live in "good" houses, and enjoy the "good" life. But what do these phrases mean? In each of them, "good" is simply used as a euphemism for pricey, for luxurious, for expensive, for upmarket. The good life is a life filled with comforts, a good job is one with high pay, and a good house is not a shack on the edge of a landfill.

It would be easy to point out that it would be far more logical to describe jobs such as nurse, or counselor, or pastoral care-worker, or teacher, or social worker as "good" jobs. These are occupations that involve providing a high level of care for others, and they also provide a high level of personal satisfaction. But these are not seen as jobs that pay big money—so modern society does not count them as "good." This is absurd, but this is the world in which we live.

***Money and status have become inexorably linked.***

Modern society seems to be set up almost deliberately in ways that confuse us. Today, it is considered wrong to tell other people—especially your workmates—how much you earn. Why? Because, if it is more than they earn, they will feel resentment, and the company stands to be damaged by waves of ill-feeling flowing through the premises. In other words, the amount you earn for doing the job you do is irrelevant. What is important is that it is at least as much as employee A, B or C, and preferably much more than D, E and F, but not as much G, H and J. The actual amount of money is irrelevant: the place in the pecking order it implies is what counts.

It was different for Siddhartha. He started life at the top of the pecking order. This meant that he already knew something that the rest of us take years to find out: that reaching a place of high rank did not lead to satisfaction. On the contrary, it merely obscured the real needs of a person. Everyone assumed that because he had a good house and a good career and lived on good food and drink that he was happy.

But he had no personal satisfaction—indeed, he had the opposite: he felt that somehow he had less than other people, and this is true. He had less knowledge of the real world. His feet were not on the ground. He had only glimpses of where real happiness lay, of what personal fulfillment was all about, of a person's place in the universe. Because he knew nothing of the real questions of life, he was actually a deprived child. And even as a youngster, he had realized this when he had had moments of lucidity, when he realized that sitting on the earth under a rose-apple tree brought more satisfaction than living in luxury in a fine home.

This can be a huge discovery, or it can come as a series of small ones. I have a friend who learned that the woman in the next office earned far more than he did: almost 50% more. Their jobs were different, and she worked far longer hours than he did. But nevertheless, he felt that the difference in pay was so enormous that he would have to do something about it. He kicked up a fuss, and at the next suitable opportunity, he was given a chance to take a post similar to hers, at the same level of pay and work. He quickly became utterly miserable. He discovered that he enjoyed his time off. He liked work, but resented having to work 60 hours a week instead of 40. The department to which he had moved was deeply stressful and staff could be called at any time of the day and night. The extra money was good, but it in no way compensated for the loss of balance in his life. He ended up apologizing to his boss and asking to be moved back to his old job. He happily went back to his old title and former salary; he earned less—but got more out of life.

***Protection from harsh reality is in itself a form of ill-treatment.***

Siddhartha's father Shuddhodana instigated a system of protectionism to prevent his son being influenced by the real world. He wanted to build layers of insulation around the boy, so that he could have full control over the development of the child's psyche, and ultimately create the successor he wanted.

But the ruler's plan backfired terribly. We can imagine that he would have been horrified at how unsuccessful his plan had been. How he had worked so hard with the boy's interests at heart, and how all he had done was create resentment. I imagine that Siddhartha's emotions toward his father would have been complex and shifting. At times, the young man would have been grateful to his father for shielding him from the horrors of the world; at other times, the young man would have been furious with him.

Yet what is clear is that the father's attempts to shelter the boy did the opposite of what was intended. This is so clear a lesson in business that it hardly needs to be expanded upon. Businesses that are protected fail to thrive. The most obvious examples are the banks and state businesses of China. Protected for decades from having to make commercial decisions in line with the real world, these businesses atrophied. They became big, over-manned processors of paperwork, and their basic function as businesses, which should have been to generate wealth, simply failed to happen. "A business without profit is no more a business than a pickle is a candy," as Charles Abbot has said. Instead, the Chinese state enterprises became job-creation centers fed by huge inputs of money from the government. They should have produced wealth; instead they became massive consumers of it.

In recent years, the state businesses of China have been going through a long process of dismantlement. This is a highly painful process, involving a complete change of culture, and tens of thousands of job losses. Yet all the problems they are going through can be blamed on an error made more than 60 years ago, when it was assumed that protecting a business was good for it.

As trade barriers fall all over the world, there has been a general realization that protectionism is a bad thing; and dismantling it is important. What has not been properly realized is the significance of removing it equitably and carefully. Abrupt or ill-managed transitions cause great pain, as Siddhartha knew. At the moment, the world is in a sorry state in which we force poorer countries to remove their protectionist laws, while allowing richer ones to maintain theirs. There are numerous examples of this, but one of the most shocking is that of world sugar production. Poor countries, such as Malawi, are made to follow anti-protectionist rules, and thus have to agree to sell sugar at market rates. Yet rich countries continue to subsidize their farmers, enabling them to flood the global market and depress sugar prices. Thus we end up with the ludicrous situation where the rich are actively using anti-protectionism laws to make the poor poorer.

Cases such as the above are sometimes used as example of why protectionism can be good. Should we not protect the people in Malawi? But what it really proves is something else: that protectionism creates ill-balanced systems, and that such systems should be dismantled over time, on all sides, and with care to ensure that as few people as possible are hurt. In some cases, the production of "fair trade" goods can work well, providing a cushion that avoids protectionism, yet enables poor farmers to get their goods to wealthy customers. The best answers are usually found from non-governmental organizations on the ground, such as Oxfam and World Vision.

The word protectionism is usually used in connection with macro-economics: the major processes by which money flows around the world. Yet it also applies to every business, large, medium or tiny. We all have markets for our goods and services. And we are all tempted to take protectionist stances to hold those markets.

Company A, for example, is a two-man outfit that produces specialist textbooks for schools. It sells directly to the schools, and so does not have to compete in the bookshops with material produced by other publishers. It has its own little protected niche. Everything seems ideal. Yet it is likely that the business will reach saturation point, and no further growth will be possible. At the same time, competitors will start selling directly to schools as well.

So what do we do? Company A needs to bite the bullet and enter the fray. It needs to sell its books in all outlets, and on the Internet, and to schools in other cities, and in other countries. If it does none of these things, it will eventually find that its protected little core market will be eaten away, its growth will disappear, and its profits will shrink. Rather than celebrate the fact that it has a small niche of its own, Company A needs to realize that it has enjoyed a good, safe, protected kick-start, but now needs to anticipate that things will get tougher. It needs to grow up and find its niche in the wider world. It needs to be Siddhartha, leaving the family home and entering the real world with all its attendant challenges.

This is a difficult thing to do. We often hear people admonishing us, telling us to leave our comfort zones. But the fact is, ambitious people spend most of their lives and the bulk of their energies building comfort zones for themselves—so they naturally don't want to leave them. We usually think of comfort zones as places or situations, but there are human elements blended in there as well. We surround ourselves with people who make us feel good. We need to get rid of them, as well, which leads to the next point.

***We surround ourselves with danger when we start hiring yes-men.***

As we move further up the ladder of success, we attract admirers. When we reach middle management, the juniors look up to us and wonder how long it would take them to reach our level. And when we reach senior management, we have a great many people in our organizations who admire us, or at least covet our seats. After all, power is an aphrodisiac: it makes us attractive.

The more powerful we become, the less likely it is that people around us will tell us the truth. This is not necessarily because they are unctuous or sycophantic. There are other reasons. They are scared of us and don't want to say the wrong thing; so they say what we want to hear, as opposed to the truth that we need to hear. Furthermore, juniors can be awed by the rich and powerful. The dynamics of conversational exchanges change, so that the boss' comments carry much more weight than the comments of juniors or ancillary staff: yet wisdom is no respecter of job titles. Human nature being what it is, it is inevitable that there will be meetings in which the wisest course is that suggested by the most junior staff member, and the least practical answers are those suggested by the seniors. In unwieldy organizations that over-respect rank, these crucial ideas from junior staff will be passed over. In well-managed organizations, staff will fail to be blinded by rank and will opt for the smart ideas, not necessarily the ones that come from the boss. What I am saying is that there are always mismatches between rank and talent. Now I hope that your organization is well managed, and your senior staff are experienced, capable individuals who are in positions of power because they deserve it. Yet in every organization there will be situations where people lower down the ladder can deliver a higher grade of truth to the meeting. Do not miss these opportunities.

I knew a manager who hired the finest designers to work on the company's new showroom. And certainly, the results were spectacular. The place looked beautiful. But one of the receptionists, after much cajoling, was persuaded to give her comments. "It's very nice to look at," she said. "But it's too nice. The customers treat it as a museum. Nobody talks to us and nobody buys anything." Within weeks it became obvious that she was right. The beauty level of the place was high and everybody cooed at it—but the customer activity level slumped. Following this, the plan was revised and the place was reconfigured to become more like a series of stalls. It was messier, but more welcoming. Customers started interacting with the shop assistants and the items on sale again. Business went up.

***Worthless suffering is surprisingly popular.***

One of the most curious things that Siddhartha discovered was the luxury of suffering. It sounds self-contradictory, but he found that people chose self-mortification for themselves because they "enjoyed" it. Depriving themselves of things gave them a perverse satisfaction. They knew that wallowing in luxury was a false route to happiness, so they tried the opposite extreme: placing themselves in positions of self-deprivation. This, Siddhartha felt, was an equally bad route to fulfillment.

There are many businesses that operate in this way, with leaders choosing suffering, not for themselves, but for their staff. These bosses feel that a group of people who work in miserable silence must be somehow better than a happy group of staff who sing as they get on with their tasks. These bosses scrimp and save on the office environment. Thick carpets and soft furnishings will make the staff too relaxed, they feel, so they go out of their way to make the environment functional. These bosses turn the air-conditioning up. Although it costs more in electricity bills, they have heard the theories that people have to be more active in cold environments, to prevent their body temperatures dropping. Also, it's good for the computers to be kept chilled. They will last longer. In many cases, this sort of attitude is not based on a study of the facts, but on a general feeling that workers will toil more energetically if they are kept on a short leash in a state of fear. Just as the Vikings whipped the slaves who rowed their boats, so bosses tongue-lash their staff. These people are skeptical about human nature, and feel that staff will skive if they are not driven harshly.

A Chinese friend of mine who worked for 10 years in Canada before being transferred to a factory in an old-fashioned part of Asia, said: "It was hard to adjust from the Canadian system, where you made staff work by encouraging them, to a system where you made staff work by threatening to humiliate them."

Bosses who organize companies like this need to get a dose of reality. Computers do thrive in chilly environments. But how long can the oldest computer work for you? Four or five years, tops, before it has to be junked and replaced? In contrast, how long can your most loyal employee work for you? Forty years? Fifty? There's no comparison. Your major assets are not machines, but human beings.

***Recognize that all that ultimately matters is internal.***

The most valuable lesson that Siddhartha brought to us is that all that matters is internal. We can have as much silver and gold as we like, and have no satisfaction whatsoever. "Better is a dish of vegetables served with love than a whole roast ox served with hate," *The Book of Proverbs* says. We need to upgrade the importance of personal satisfaction in our work lives, and downgrade the focus on financial rewards. Conversely, by moving the focus off money, our companies become happier, healthier places; they function better; they become more creative; and in the end, yes, they make more money.

## LIFE ON THE ROAD

THE THOUGHTS AND ideas Siddhartha had during this period have been categorized into various lists and articles of faith, generally known as the *dharma*—yes, the word we have already encountered several times. He drew a wheel, which became his symbol. For practical purposes, what seems to have happened is that he was re-joined by the five companions who had been searching for the truth with him. At the Deer Park near Varanasi, he told them about the Middle Way he had found. His friends—who now should more accurately be called his followers—started to refer to him as the Awakened One: in Sanskrit, the *Buddha*.

Over the next 45 years, he and his companions traveled around northeastern India, refining and teaching his doctrine, and demonstrating his discipline to a range of people, from high-ranking nobles to low-caste road sweepers. Don't be indulgent and don't be ascetic, the Awakened One said. If you are unhappy, realize that you don't have to be. The unhappiness of suffering is caused by cravings. If you don't crave things, you won't suffer from unhappiness. You can control your cravings. You can stop them. And there is more that you should do: look inside yourself first, then look outside. After learning to do no harm to yourself, learn that you should do no harm to other human beings. Furthermore, learn to do no harm to any living creature.

He was not a writer, but it appears that he made his teaching easier to take in and memorize (there were no leaflets to hand out or books to distribute) by turning his principles into numbered lists: the four noble truths, the noble eight-fold path and so on.

The teaching was popular, and the number of followers grew from dozens to hundreds, and then started to creep into the thousands. But at this stage, Siddhartha's philosophy was nothing like a world religion. It was merely a teaching from an unusual un-religious teacher.

At the age of 80, Siddhartha fell ill after eating a dish, said to be pork, given as an offering from a blacksmith named Cunda. As he became increasingly ill, he is said to have told his disciples not to tell Cunda that his cooking was responsible. Siddhartha wanted the blacksmith's good intentions to be placed higher than the cruel reality of the fact that there were pathogens in the food. He died shortly afterwards and was cremated, with the bones of his body being sent as relics to *stupas* around the region.

Many went to Magadha, a place we know well, and which we are about to re-enter.

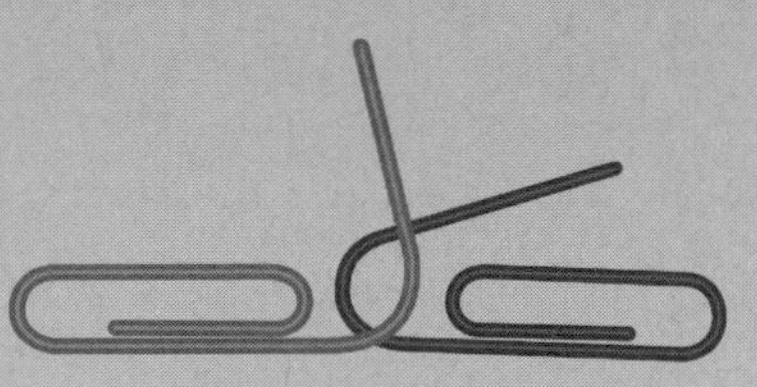

# THE CAPACITY TO CHANGE THE WORLD

7

**A LEADER WITH A HUGE AMOUNT OF DRIVE USES IT FOR BOTH GOOD AND EVIL, AND RECORDS HIS FINDINGS IN THE EXTRAORDINARY – *EDICTS OF ASHOKA*.**

## A KING'S BLOODY REIGN

AS SO OFTEN happens, brilliance in a family sometimes skips a generation or two. While Bindusara, the "untimely ripped" son of Chandragupta Maurya, did not lose his father's empire, neither did he achieve much in expanding it. He possibly added a portion of the south-central regions of the subcontinent to the empire, but did little else to make his name ring through the ages, except for one incidental contribution: he fathered a child who grew to become possibly the most celebrated leader that India ever had.

His name was Ashoka and he was the king who ruled with his sword. Apparently a violent man with a capacity for achievement, he seemed to have the drive and passion that turned his grandfather into Chandragupta Maurya the Unstoppable.

The young prince had no doubt heard many times the stories of how his grandfather, the peacock tamer's boy, had started with nothing, but had ousted the Nanda dynasty, taken over Magadha and expanded the empire to cover the northern half of India and much of the central region. He would have heard how his grandfather's army had conquered kingdom after kingdom, how Chandragupta had defeated the heirs of Alexander the Great, and how he worked with the great sage Kautilya Chanakya to expand the kingdom in all directions as far as they could go.

When Bindusara died, his sons battled to take over the kingdom. Ashoka won the battle, confirming his grasp on the throne with his sword: the story goes that he killed 99 half-brothers. He probably did kill a few, and maybe a great many, given what else we are told about his personality. Looking at his life, one gets the impression that the new king was much like his grandfather in at least two ways. He was a soldier, and a particularly tough and merciless one. He apparently built a torture chamber that was so horrible that people said he had descended to Hell itself to pick up design ideas. This room was a fabled tourist attraction in India for centuries, before it was lost. And second, he had a latent spiritual streak, just like his grandfather. He looked for portents in the heaven and he became increasingly intrigued by the Buddhists and the Jains crisscrossing his kingdom. Ashoka was believed to have had a couple of great loves in his life, one of whom was a young woman who was a member of the Awakened.

While Bindusara may have made incursions into central and South India, he had lost or failed to hold on to Kalinga, a large region of forested land in East India inhabited by tough warrior tribes. His son Ashoka is said to have expanded the kingdom further, although historical evidence exists for only one battle: the fight for Kalinga. He seemed to have had his grandfather's talent for conquest. He no doubt used Chanakya's books for advice and followed the military techniques perfected by his grandfather. They still worked—and Ashoka, who seemed to be a more steely man than either his father or grandfather, hacked away to maintain and enlarge the country.

Staring at the map of his territory, Ashoka evidently started to become obsessive about Kalinga—the one spot on the map that seemed Maurya-proof. Every time he had taken over a new state, he had absorbed extra men and weapons, his army becoming increasingly powerful. He had also, the stories suggest, become more violent.

The day came when he decided he would have to take Kalinga using extreme force. He set out his orders. A massive army would pour into the stronghold on multiple fronts and kill every man and every war animal, horse or elephant. All women and children would be taken prisoners. There would be no mercy.

The people of Kalinga, proud of being independent, fought bravely. But theirs was a forlorn hope. The powerful army of invaders carved their way into the city. At the end of the battle, it is said that the streets were lined with bodies, and the river at the heart of the town ran red with blood. The number of people of Kalinga who lay dead at the end of the battle was estimated (by Ashoka's men) at 100,000. And more than that number died later of wounds and disease. The bodies of horses and elephants also lined the city streets.

With that win, Ashoka's kingdom included much of what is today's India, probably missing only the southernmost portion. It was the largest united India the world had ever seen, and it was to remain an unbroken record for two millennia, until the British arrived. In size, it was one of the greatest empires in the world.

Emperor Ashoka marched into the devastated capital of Kalinga in victory, the story goes. It must have been a grisly scene, the river banks lined with corpses. Bodies rot fast in India, and his visit must have been during the brief window before the place became noxious and disease-ridden. One imagines that any feeling of triumph he and his generals felt would have been somewhat tempered by the horror of the scene.

Suddenly, something stirred at the water's edge. It was a disheveled figure of some sort, carrying a bundle. The mythologists have turned the figure into a monk, and some say it was a reincarnation of Siddhartha Gautama himself. But these embellishments are unnecessary. I prefer to think of it as an ordinary citizen of Kalinga. Given the army's orders to kill all males, it was probably a female.

"You are a mighty king," the figure said, or words to that effect. "You are the emperor. You are a god. You alone have been responsible for the deaths of 100,000 people."

How did Ashoka react? Was he proud? Was he unnerved? What did his guards do? I imagine they would initially have been suspicious of the grim character approaching from the river, but would perhaps have relaxed somewhat on hearing her words of praise for the conqueror. "O god-emperor, you have taken away the lives of one hundred thousand people," she said. "Now show us that you truly are Ashoka the all-powerful. Give back the life of just one: this child."

In my mind's eye, I see the disheveled woman throw the bundle toward the emperor. He, of course, is disgusted, and has no interest in catching it. Perhaps the broken body of the child lands on the ground between them. The name of the woman and the child are not recorded. The only name we have to go with the story is the name of the river. It was changed to the

River Daya, meaning the River of Compassion—a name it still carries today.

But nevertheless, that exchange, whether it took place in the form that tradition has recorded, or in quite different circumstances, or largely in the head of Ashoka or one of his biographers, had a profound effect on the emperor, the evidence of which remains all over India, millennia afterward. All the historical data show a complete transformation in the behavior and attitude of the violent king from roughly then onward. Whatever happened in Kalinga, it broke Ashoka's heart. He returned to his home in Magadha, pondering over what he had seen. And when he next emerged from the palace, he was a different man.

Incursions by his armies into other people's lands halted immediately. Ashoka made a statement announcing that he was making a 180-degree turn in his aims and objectives. He looked for a new philosophy to drive him, and he found it.

For some years already, his kingdom had been receptive to the growing presence of the Awakened, even at the highest levels of society. Ashoka already knew about the man who had asked the central question that all men, subconsciously, were trying to find the answer to: *How should a man live?* He would have known that Siddhartha of the Sakya Clan himself had visited the royal palace in Magadha more than a century earlier, and how his philosophy of being enlightened had become a leading code of belief, along with the Jain system that Mahavira had introduced. But while there was a harsh, extreme austerity about the Jains—whose doctrines had inspired his grandfather to starve himself to death—the Awakened were said to be the calmest, most other-worldly, least violent human beings in the known world.

Ashoka summoned teachers of the Awakened to the palace and buried himself in learning. He was truly reborn. So was his philosophy. And so was his country. He announced that a new principle would drive his huge empire: *dhamma* (a

Prakit word meaning "pious behavior," closely related to the Sanskrit word *dharma*). This was a pro-peace philosophy that would turn the strictures of the Buddhists and the Jains, such as *ahimsa*, meaning "non-violence," into a way of governing. "Instead of the sound of the war drum, the sound of *dhamma* will be heard," the emperor said. Ashoka adopted the wheel of Siddhartha as the symbol of the new India—and it can still be seen at the heart of the Indian flag. At some stage, he adopted a new name: Piyadassi, which had overtones of kindness and graciousness. But it is suspected that no one referred to him by either of his names: at such an exalted rank, he was spoken of only as the Beloved of the Gods.

Having conquered all the neighboring territories, Ashoka Piyadassi, the Beloved of the Gods, embarked on an extraordinary mission: to conquer the future. So convinced was he of the benefits of the new way of life, that he wanted these principles to survive him, and his children, and the future generation. He wanted to make them eternal. So he started on the most extraordinary writing program that any ancient leader ever undertook. He started dictating a sort of diary, a record of his thoughts and acts and achievements, which were to be carved into the very face of the country—a sort of stone blog, if you like. Historians refer to them as edicts, but this is misleading: they are not neat lists of laws and statutes, and their language is not formal or rhythmical. They come across as first person speech—indeed, in places they have an intimate feel, almost as if they were rock-carved transcripts of recordings. The writings are rambling and somewhat repetitive. In content, they are news reports, often rather self-serving, keeping the people informed about what their emperor was up to and his thoughts as he continued to implement *dhamma* as a form of governance. He slips between first person and third person speech, just as one would expect a human with god-like status to do.

Reading these notes, one can see him pacing around the room at his palace in Pataliputra, his eyes in the middle distance, as he dictated his thoughts out loud. He spoke about his remorse for what had happened in Kalinga, and said that behaving correctly, with goodness and love, was the most important thing. "This world and the other are hard to gain without great love of righteousness, great self-examination, great obedience, great circumspection, great effort," he said. "For this is my rule, to govern by righteousness, to administer by righteousness, to please my subjects by righteousness, and to protect them by righteousness." His utterances would have been taken down verbatim by scribes working on palm-leaf paper of some sort. And then they were taken to the masons to be carved into rock.

His message was clear: "The sound of the war-drum has been replaced by the sound of the *dhamma*." Many historians believe that the conversion of the Roman Emperor Constantine to Christianity was a key step in turning a small cult into a world religion. The same has been said for Emperor Ashoka's embracing of Buddhism. It took the next step toward becoming the major faith in a huge and influential empire. And just as he had dispatched warriors in all directions, the emperor started dispatching missionaries to spread words of peace and forbearance. He sent his son and daughter as peaceful emissaries of the Awakened way to what is now Sri Lanka, and scored an astonishing success in converting the island people to the new faith. He sent people to spread the word to Greece and Egypt and countries in between. Their message was that Ashoka wished all beings could have "security, self-control, calmness of mind, and gentleness." But having said that, he was no Buddhist missionary—he was the missionary of *dhamma*. He didn't mention the Buddha in any of his letters to his people, and many of his thoughts on protecting animals probably came from Jainism. He seemed to be trying to absorb all that was good in the codes of behavior around him, and to encapsulate them into a revolutionary form of governance.

The violent Ashoka had become the King of Peace. His 40-year reign (273 BCE to 232 BCE) became a remarkably peaceful time. He introduced a free health care system. He spent the money in his coffers on building hospitals, medical dispensaries, and even hospices for the dying. These places had a voluntary code of payment. If you had money, you could pay. If you had none, you received treatment at no cost. He was so devoted to health care that he established distribution systems to send information and medicines to neighboring kingdoms, including Lanka and Greece. Where medicinal plants did not grow, he sent gardeners with fruits and seeds and roots to cultivate them. "I consider my work to be the welfare of the whole world," he said. "There is no better deed than to work for the welfare of the whole world and all my efforts are made that I may clear my debt to all beings."

Anticipating later Indian (and still later Western) thought, he became acutely aware of the rights of animals—especially the right of wild animals not to be eaten. He banned animal sacrifice and established free animal hospitals, paying the salaries of veterinarians himself. Ashoka became what we would think of today as an environmentalist. He urged his people to respect what nature had provided and banned any activity that would pollute water sources. He transferred all responsibility for maintaining the forests to the purse of the state. "Moreover I have had banyan trees planted on the roads to give shade to man and beast; I have planted mango groves, and I have had ponds dug up and shelters erected along the roads at every eight kilometers. Everywhere I have had wells dug for the benefit of man and beast," he wrote.

The kitchens that fed the emperor's staff had been slaughtering several hundred thousand animals a day. He banned the practice. (Although, somewhat comically, he is so honest that he has to admit that the kitchens cannot do without killing three creatures—two peacocks and a deer—every day, although he pledges to wean them off the practice eventually.) Some people believe India became a vegetarian state, while others think he banned the killing of wild animals but not farmed animals. Certainly, India even today contains a large proportion of the world's vegetarians.

Ashoka sent *dhamma* officers to speak to people in the prisons. Their job was to rehabilitate prisoners, working toward the day when they could be released back into society. There could be a variety of reasons to release people from jail—"Perhaps they are old or have a family to support," he wrote.

He decided to make a pilgrimage to thank the spirit of Siddhartha for what he had learned. Accompanied by a retinue of thousands of royal courtiers, plus 18,000 members of the Awakened, Ashoka visited Siddhartha's home. He went to the Awakened One's birthplace in Kapilavastu, the spot where he renounced his life of indulgence, the tree in the town of Gaya where he was first awakened, and to the Deer Park where the Awakened One told his friends about the principles that governed his new philosophy. There, Ashoka erected a pillar crowned with four lions facing the four points of the compass (then thought of as "the four corners of the world"), denoting that spiritual and societal peace would radiate in all directions from India outward. That's the pillar now displayed on India's flag. On the pillar underneath, masons carved one of Ashoka's letters.

Perhaps the most remarkable thing about the emperor's conversion to his personal *dhamma* brand of Buddhism is that he managed to be passionate about it while respecting other religions: a state of tolerance that seems very modern, smacking of today's multi-faith meetings. His twelfth rock letter says: "Whoever honors his own sect and disparages another man's, whether from blind loyalty or with the intention of showing his own sect in a favorable light, does his own sect the greatest possible harm. Concord is best, with each hearing and respecting the other's teachings."

The masons carved his words into rocks and pillars, and transported them all over his kingdom, even setting some up in neighboring countries. Ashoka quite literally caused his humanitarian philosophy to be carved into the face of his country.

Passionate, intelligent, whole-hearted Ashoka, the ultimate driven man, turned India into a nation built on advanced principles that were thousands of years ahead of their time.

## MEASURING YOUR CAPACITY

BEFORE THE QUESTION of how good or how bad you are comes a different question: how driven are you? From a brief examination of Ashoka's life, most people think that his is a tale of transformation: he seems to have two completely different personalities, with the slaughter at Kalinga being the point at which he changed from one to the other.

But in fact we can see that there was one overriding quality that ran through his entire life: he was the ultimate driven man. When he was wielding a sword, he was using it to change the lives of hundreds of thousands of people by adding towns, cities and regions to his empire at speed. When he was wielding an olive branch, he once again spread it over a huge area—his own expanded country, and those of his neighbors. He "invaded" his neighbors' countries to deliver plants and medicines. Ashoka was a man of enormous vision and self-belief. Furthermore, he seemed to have no concept of personal boundaries. He was a citizen of the world. There was only one world, and one species of human being. These facts seemed self-evident to him, and tribalism was ultimately absurd. If he wanted to send something out to the people, he sent it to his own people and everyone within reach beyond his borders.

What he had that made him stand out above the other rulers at that time was *capacity*. Whatever fired him, he grasped with both hands. He must have had an unbelievable amount of energy and confidence. He comes across as a man hungry for achievement and who had an astonishing capacity to make his dreams into reality. This is curious, given the fact that he was brought up ensconced in wealth and splendor. The children of today's leaders, whether they have royal blood, elected mandates, or are merely the offspring of business leaders or movie stars, so often allow their lives to dissipate. They have never been hungry, so they do not develop the drive that hunger brings. Raised in a world of privilege, they become convinced that they somehow deserve it. A media that is increasingly focused on the worship of celebrity and wealth reinforces this. And we end up making role models of people who do not even have the capacity to fix themselves, let alone the world.

Ashoka had that drive, he had that energy, and he had an unquenchable desire to alter the world: and change it he did. It manifested itself in three ways: in the power of his military leadership; in the way he took in the slaughter at Kalinga and allowed it to change his life; and in the manner of which he became the apostle of *dhamma*.

These days, modern people often try to locate what drives them. At school and at university, we have career counselors who attempt to pinpoint our key motivators; there are written tests and pop quizzes that focus on the desires that drive us. And some of the oldest tests, such as the Enneagram, are among the most successful at identifying the elements that drive us. Yet the question that is not asked is this: you may know what drives you, but *how much* drive do you have? How much capacity do you have? How much energy do you have?

I know several people who love movies and have great skill in dissecting a film over dinner: they know what makes a good movie work, and can quickly locate the source of the problems in a flawed one. Several of them harbor the ambition to write or direct their own screenplays. But I doubt that any of them will make it. The talent may well be there: but to become a major creative force in the movie business you don't just need to have the ability to analyze movies—unless you are a family member of a major player, you need unbelievable amounts of drive. It's a terrifyingly competitive business, with few winners. Unless you display that hunger from morning till night, preferably from an early age, you are unlikely to make it. Steven Spielberg made his first film for cinema release at the age of 21. George Lucas's first full-length film was based on a short he had shot as a student at college. Robert Rodríguez of *Spy Kids* fame shot movies as a child, editing them by connecting two video tape recorders and juggling tapes. These people, and their contemporaries such as Martin Scorsese and James Cameron, all had talent. But it wasn't just their skill that got them to the top of their chosen field: they had huge amounts of drive. From their earliest days, they knew what they wanted and went out to get it. Some had good connections, some did not. Some had money, some didn't. Some lived in California, others didn't (Rodríguez was raised in Mexico and Cameron is from Canada). But they all shared the capacity to get where they wanted to be.

It's a sad truth that we all go through our lives meeting people with ambitions that we know will never be realized. Person A would like to leave his employment and set up his own business; Person B dreams of working with her idol, famous business leader C; Person D works on play scripts in her spare time, but never finishes them. Probably every reader knows people like this. Ambitious dreams are two a penny. We all have them at one time or another. And people who read business-themed books almost definitely have them in spades. But we, the truly ambitious, know that having the dream is not enough. There is no guarantee that it will get you anywhere except into ever deeper circles of frustration. What makes the difference is our capacity to make them real.

How do we develop that capacity? How do we make sure we have enough drive and energy to make our visions become realities?

There are three key steps we need to take. First, we need to take our dream from where it started—from its initial state as an idea, floating on top of our consciousness—and take it deep into our hearts. It needs to be at the very core of our being. It needs to be so dominant that it is always there, we are tempted to talk about it all the time, and sometimes we come across as obsessive and single-minded. Bit by bit, taking this step will change who you are. People will no longer think of you as a trainee accountant, or an insurance salesperson. They will instead identify you with your dream: "He's a filmmaker, always out on shoots or trying to raise money. At the same time, he's sensibly keeping his day job in an office until he's got a firmer footing in the movie industry." Instead of being someone who works in an office and dreams of being in movies, be someone who is in the movie business but is temporarily sojourning in a cubicle.

Second, we have to take the desire to succeed from the core of our beings and let it flood out into the rest of our lives. It must be just under the surface at all times. Instead of feeling jealous that someone else has good contacts, we should realize that we all meet a variety of people through our lives: there will almost definitely be useful contacts you can use. Use the six degrees principle. Someone you know will know someone who knows someone who knows someone who knows Jerry Bruckheimer or

Jackie Chan. If enough people know what you want, they can get you a meeting with The Man Himself, whoever that man or woman might be in your chosen field.



But when you finally make it to the room with the person who can make your dreams come true, how do you approach him? How do you work up the courage to bring up the subject? What do you say? If your dream is always with you, bubbling under the surface and driving you, you will have no trouble doing this. It will give you the courage to talk to the people to whom you need to speak; and it will put the right words into your mouth. You will find yourself doing an elevator-pitch fluently and passionately. You won't need to rehearse. It will burst from your mouth: "I'm Jane, and I've been developing a new entertainment concept that has test-marketed incredibly successfully. I'd love to share it with you."

You'll find that it won't just be the quality of the idea that grabs that person's attention. It will be your energy level. If you come across as an enthusiastic, focused, driven person who appears dead set to achieve your goal, that business leader will want a slice of the action. And you may well find that it isn't the product he wants a slice of. If you show that you have a huge capacity to succeed, what he will really want is a slice of you.

Thirdly, allow others to share in your vision. It's hard to maintain a dream by yourself. If you have internalized your mission and can truly come across as someone who is set to succeed, it will be easy to find people who want to join you. Ambitious business people should learn to think of the word "encourage" in its original French sense: *in courage*. Members of the team will need to feed each other's inner courage.

Furthermore, when you share your dream, you will multiply your business contacts. If you don't bump into the right person in the elevator or at a cocktail party, one of your teammates will. Or better still, you will both approach him or her from multiple angles, and that person will think there really is a "hot" idea bubbling under the surface, coming at him from all sides.

So share both your idea and your enthusiasm. Become a team of 10 people speaking with one voice. This doesn't mean that you should give your idea away. You can stay as CEO, or skipper, or helmsman of the team. But speaking with 10 voices will always create a louder buzz than speaking with one. Surprisingly, when I talk to entrepreneurs at conferences and training sessions, they find it hard to share their ambitions. As I said earlier, business people tend to be control freaks of the worst sort. This is not really surprising, since they know that getting the details right is one of the keys to success. So they will write the press release, they will do the interviews, they will write the work manual. But this inevitably causes problems in two ways. First, everything slows down, because one person is doing all the key jobs. And second, the team energy is not building up, so no buzz is being created. So cut lose. Drop your reserve. Tell yourself six times every morning: I will not be a control freak today. Empower your staff and colleagues. Share your enthusiasm with them, and when they are as fired up as you are, unleash them on the world.

***Be flexible enough to change direction—even if it means turning 180 degrees.***

There are few people who have changed their lives as dramatically as Ashoka of the Maurya Clan. He spread violence for years, and then spread peace for years. His is an object lesson for us in these days where several countries still believe in non-redemptive forms of punishment, the death penalty and so on. These concepts are powered by a failure to understand that people have different amounts of energy, and that they can and should be re-channeled in a positive way.

But one thing that Ashoka did was very unusual for a leader who made his reputation on his ruthlessness and single-mindedness. He admitted he was wrong. Not only did he throw out his old policies, but he devoted the rest of his life to making sure that everyone knew that he had got it wrong and had changed his ways.

I've seen feature articles recommending that leaders "should never say sorry." They promote the myth that being strong means being inflexible. They promote the image of the traditional macho man, who would rather drive for a thousand miles in the wrong direction than to lower himself to actually wind down the window and ask for directions. This strong, tough, dumb image of the leader is one that has never been true. Good leaders have always been the most flexible ones. If you ask people what Charles Darwin came up with, they will always say that he came up with the concept of the "survival of the fittest." In fact, he didn't say that. If you go back to his book, he wrote that survival does NOT go to the strongest or the cleverest or the fastest, but to the most adaptable. It is the ability to adapt to our circumstances, and to change direction—whatever it costs—that divides the winners from the losers. It is the key principle in the evolution of life, according to Darwin. And it is the key principle in successfully leading an organization, too.

It's been wisely said that "it takes a real man to apologize." It's a good thing to do for more than one reason. First, it establishes you as an honest and human individual. It's actually very difficult for a business leader to get a public reputation as a live human being. People are jealous of rich corporate chiefs and will naturally refuse to give them the benefit of any doubt. It's a piece of cake for a business boss to become known as an aloof and hard-hearted taskmaster. But to be known as a human being who once got it wrong and apologized for it creates a different image entirely—one that spinmasters and public relations executives would find very hard to build with press releases.

Second, apologizing allows one to get over things and move on. This is important in business these days, where there are always too many things to get done and never enough time and mental energy to do them all. A few months ago, two business partners of my acquaintance fell out. One apologized profusely for any shortcomings of his own and invited the other to go out with him for dinner and movie. The invitation was declined. No sweat. An apology and reconciliation had been offered. The man had done what he needed to do, and got on with his life. The other took a severely self-righteous attitude, refused to apologize for anything, and declined any offers of social contact or reconciliation. You could just see him burning up with bitterness and anger. It was interesting: although there were almost definitely faults on both sides, only one of the pair had admitted to having any shortcomings, yet he was the one who had the happy ending. It's an unusual tactic to take in this day and age, but it really works, and is a useful key to recovering from quarrels and arguments: he who apologizes first, wins. That's because the person who apologizes is the one who is setting the past where it needs to be—behind you both—and focusing on the area that deserves one's attention: the now.

***The key to the functioning of an organization is found in a leader's personal qualities.***

When a major figure undergoes some sort of scandal, there is always a big debate about the separation between a person's private life and their functions at work. The most notable recent example was probably the legendary infidelities of former US President Bill Clinton in the 1990s, although there are numerous other examples, such as the private life of Francois Mitterrand of France, who was found, at his funeral, to have had a secret mistress and love child.

The revelation of these incidents are automatically followed by op-ed articles in the newspapers pointing out that many people considered celebrated leaders (J.F. Kennedy is invariably trotted out by lazy feature-writers as an example) had a gross inability to maintain society's values in their private lives. If they govern the country well, what difference does it make if their personal lives are in a mess? These features are often written with a rather strident tone that makes one suspect they are generated by a feeling of guilt. I can't help but wonder about the private lives of some of the op-ed writers on our newspapers!

Even the most cursory reading of history shows that a person's private life and public life are indelibly connected. When Ashoka was a man of violence, so was his kingdom. When he became a man of peace, so India flowered as a place of advanced peacetime thinking in many fields. The leader is the model for the led.

Of course, society's values change. Ashoka had several wives—and Bill Clinton would no doubt have fitted better into that kind of system. But in those days, that was the norm. In today's society, we go by today's rules. And with regards to the Clinton situation, one cannot help but feel that a man who tells untruths to his wife and child—to people who really should be his nearest and dearest—simply cannot be trusted by anyone else. It's obvious: if you lie to your family, there is no one to whom you cannot tell a lie. If a leader can mislead his child, then he can never be trusted by his employees or his rivals or his board members. And an individual who behaves in a way that suggests that he doesn't care whether his own family is hurt or humiliated, doesn't inspire confidence that he genuinely cares about his staff or, in the case of a political leader, the millions of families he has never met. Or to put it another way, a man who gets the most powerful job in the world, but finds that it doesn't demand enough interest to inspire him to keep his trouser zipper up for four years, does not have his heart in his work.

## THE CODE BREAKER

THE MAN WHO CRACKED the most important code in Indian historical research was neither a code-cracker nor a historian. He made money in the most literal sense: he worked at the mint in British Calcutta in the 1830s. But James Prinsep was an enthusiastic amateur historian, and he managed to puzzle out something that had baffled people for centuries.

Pondering over undeciphered writing on the stone railings of a Buddhist *stupa,* he worked out, letter by letter, that the writing was an ancient form of Pali, as used in Magadha, more than 2,000 years ago. After months spent over transcripts of the symbols, he managed to translate a text that had probably not been read for hundreds of years. Hearing of his success, historians from all over India sent him copies of text they too had found on rocks and had never been able to translate.

At first, there did not seem to be anything to link this large collection of carvings. Some were on cliff faces, others on pillars polished till they were shiny, still others on large rocks. Eventually, other similar inscriptions were found that were in different languages.

Prinsep announced he had cracked the code in 1837. The historians that followed him eventually translated all of them. They were very old writings, and seemed to contain an extraordinary series of letters from a man who called himself Beloved of the Gods, King Piyadassi. The messages were almost unbelievable: the carvings were very old indeed, harking back to the years before Christ, yet the sentiments they carried seemed like modern humanitarian thought. But there was no Piyadassi in any historical records of Indian kings. Who left the mysterious diary, carved in rock over the surface of India?

The clue that linked the names came from what is now Sri Lanka, where ancient Buddhist sources told the story of "Ashoka known as Piyadassi," the great Indian king who sent his children to bring Buddhism to the island. Gradually, using those and other sources, the full story of Ashoka was carefully uncovered. But the "rock edicts" remain the primary source—a unique series of intimate letters from a highly enlightened ruler of the past.

Analysis of the material revealed that these really were letters, in the sense that they were written and then "posted" and delivered. The emperor had hired teams of masons to carve them onto the finest stone, quarried from a place called Chunar, 100 miles south of Varanasi. To make sure the message would get further than India's borders, he had them translated into several languages, including Aramaic and Greek, the languages of Jesus and the New Testament authors. They were erected in India, Nepal, Pakistan and Afghanistan. Time passed, and the Beloved of the Gods was forgotten. The language of the rocks became archaic, and was eventually forgotten all together. The stories of King Piyadassi were lost to history, until Prinsep's remarkable decoding feat started a flurry of discovery.

Ashoka, who had disappeared from history, has since been returned to prominence. Independent India's first prime minister, Jawaharlal Nehru, used his symbol of four lions as the symbol of India, and the wheel at its center became the centerpiece of the flag of India. That Buddhist wheel that Ashoka promoted appears on Indian coins today. His reign has been celebrated as one of the most enlightened on earth. He is fêted in story and song all over India, and to some extent, outside. The British writer H.G. Wells described him as "the greatest of kings." Movies have been made of his life.

Ashoka, in the first part of his life, conquered Kalinga and other lands. But in the second part of his life he successfully managed to place his mark of peace on most of the subcontinent, plus a far, far more difficult place to reach: the distant future, more than two thousand years after his death.

Now that's what I call a man with the capacity to get his message across. He would no doubt have been delighted. One of his statements, found on a rock, was: "All men are my children."

# 8 ACHIEVING BALANCE

**A YOUNG MAN EMBARKS ON A MISSION TO SUMMARIZE AND CODIFY HUMAN RELATIONSHIPS AND PRODUCES THE *KAMA SUTRA*.**

## THE RELIGIOUS STUDENT

IT IS ONE OF those unbelievable-but-true factoids that you can throw into dinner party conversations: that the most successful book on sex ever written was authored by a young student of religion—and that he was celibate.

Yes, it is hard to believe, and yes, we ought to find out more about him. Yet there are very few hard facts available about this author, or how he came to write one of the most famous books of all time. But there is one way of knowing his character: his personality shines out of the single work that made him famous throughout history—the *Kama Sutra*.

His name was Vatsyayana and he lived about 16 centuries ago; we can't be much more precise than that. The work itself is not provided with a date, and no indisputable conclusions have been made by people trying to work out the provenance of the book from clues found within its text. Scholars vacillate around the third and fourth century CE. Some sources give him the first name Mallanaga, but others claim that name belongs to a separate individual. His name is often shortened to Vatsyana and even Vatsya—so we'll go with the last of those, since it is a short, neat and very Indian.

Vatsya was a bookworm. He was a scholar of religion, probably based at a university in Varanasi, a city considered not just holy, but the actual gateway between heaven and earth. In Western culture, it would be equivalent to the cloud where St. Peter sits holding a bunch of keys in front of the Pearly Gates. This city is the place where bodies of the dead are cremated for their final journey along the sacred River Ganges. Little has changed over the centuries, and even today, Varanasi retains its gateway-to-the-other-world status. It is considered particularly auspicious to be born or to die in the city, so the road into town is lined with two sets of people, both of whom walk with great difficulty: the very old and the very pregnant. In Varanasi, you certainly get the feel that the human circle of life is in very obvious, visible operation.

Vatsya became interested in the big body of collected writings known as the *kamashastra*, or the "treatise on pleasure." (This is not to be confused with the *Kama Sutra*, the book Vatsya eventually wrote.) The *kamashastra* was a very large collection of books and scrolls to be found in the libraries of the best universities, including the one where he was studying. There was no shame for a young man to take an interest in such matters in those days. Erotic lore was not despised in the way pornography is in most places these days, although it is clear from other writings that there was a general feeling that taking too much interest in such things was unhealthy. It appears that he was not married or employed, but "entirely" devoted to the study of God.

Where does this information come from? Much of it comes from tradition, but there are clear references in the text that support it. The text itself is straightforward and unfanciful, and in it, Vatsya clearly appears to indicate that he is a religious student, and it was thus likely that he was not an old man (although, like his first English translator Sir Richard Burton, we may decide that he was far too worldly-wise be in the first flush of youth). Vatsya says his energy is "entirely devoted to contemplation of the Almighty," which seems to reinforce the celibacy claim. Indeed, the whole picture presented by the book is an image of a rather open-minded person in a religious department of a university, writing his notes as he engages in discussions about the place of *kama* (pleasure) in the balance of other key elements of life, including *dharma* (virtue) and *artha* (material wealth). This is almost exactly the same issue that was a prime focus for Chanakya, the first personality featured in this book.

Furthermore, there is no indication that the work recorded activities that Vatsya personally researched; on the contrary, it is made clear that he is a compiler, assembling other people's work, not in any way an experienced man writing a sexual autobiography—he is no Henry Miller. For example, the text does sometimes veer toward impracticalities, suggesting that the writer failed to personally test the ideas in the book. As a case in point, he appears very unsure about how female orgasm works, and seems to think that a mixture of male semen and "female semen" is emitted during sex, and is the trigger for reproduction. But this naivety is more than balanced by his sophistication in interpersonal relationships. Despite living 1,600 years ago, Vatsya argued the very modern view that sex was not just a system for making babies; it was enjoyable for its own sake. (We can forgive him his ignorance on the mechanics of reproduction. The only widely accepted view at that time, and for centuries afterward, was the one Aristotle came up with almost 2,500 years ago—that women produced the physical material for the new baby, and men produced the "life force" that animated it, which helped it start growing.)

Unlike many of the other influential Indians in this book, Vatsya was no innovator. He was following a well-trodden path. However, innovations are often but better copies of originals. The field of *kamashastra* was already well established, and had attracted the attention of many scholars before him. But the difference between this scholar and other men curious about the books of carnal knowledge in the university library was this: he and he alone, it seems, recognized that there was enormous value in sifting through this massive body of material and re-shaping it in a form that the wider community could read. He wanted to make it accessible. He wanted to bring it a bigger audience. He wanted to add value by taking away bulk. He was what we would call today a re-packager.

With this thought in the back of his mind, he started reading the totality of the information with a view to making a précis of it. Like any good modern researcher, he knew that the first step would be to fully comprehend historical and present-day thinking about his chosen field so that he could summarize it and move the debate forward. The first thing he discovered was that he was not the only person who had the idea of making the erotic lore accessible. There were other books summarizing this information in existence, some of which were said to be very comprehensive and which had been famous for decades or centuries.

He found copies of them, from his university or at other universities. It turned out that none of the books—or at least none that he had managed to obtain—was the same as the one he was envisaging. None was short, practical and accessible. Indeed, the more he researched, the more Vatsya must have become convinced that his idea was a winner. Relationships and sexuality were such a huge part of human life. A book that neatly summarized the wide amount of information circulating on the subject could only be a success.

He did his initial research thoroughly, and we can surmise that he must have been amazed at the sheer scale of what he discovered. His first sources were the senior religious teachers and librarians at his hall of learning. From them he learned that the compilation of facts about love and pleasure dated right back to the beginning of time. The Lord of Being laid down the complete rules of existence in a set of books that was over 100,000 chapters long, the legends stated. No one had the full version of this massive tome, but individual human beings in history had been given responsibility of compiling specialist sections of the work on certain themes. For example, the section on *dharma* was compiled by one Swayambhu Manu. The chapters that related to *artha* were handled by a man named Brihaspati. And the section in which he was interested, the section on *kama*, which can be translated as sensual pleasure, was compiled by Nandi, the sacred bull, in one document, 1,000 chapters long. It was said that Nandi had been inspired to compile separately the holy wisdom about love after overhearing the love-making of two gods.

Nandi's thousand-chapter book of love being too lengthy to be of general use, it was abridged and summarized by a human: Shvetaketu, son of Uddvalaka. This man boiled the cow-god's work down to a mere 500 chapters. But it soon became evident that this also was too long for general use. And so the summary itself was summarized by one Babhravya, a man who we learn had inherited land south of Delhi, and thus presumably lived off rental income while he did his editing. He slashed and burned the text until he had got it down to a mere 150 chapters.

Vatsya managed to get a copy of Babhravya's book, although there were no complete copies of the earlier works, especially the one written by the sacred bull. But the student continued to follow the trail, and found that the editing process had changed direction after Babhravya. Until his version, the "selected highlights" had been shrinking. But after him, the compilation of love lore started to grow again. Babhravya's 150-chapter book was edited into seven parts, divided by themes: On the Art of Seduction, On Dealing with One's Wife, On Dealing with the Wives of Others, On Courtesans, and so on. These sections were separated and given to seven scholars to interpret and compose commentaries on. Each had turned their section into a book in itself.

Vatsya painstakingly collected copies of as many of these works as possible. The difficulty he had in amassing the pile of material, and reading through it, would have further convinced him that he was on the right track. It would be good to have "a small volume as an abstract of the works of the above named authors," he wrote in his notes.

## WRITING A CLASSIC

EVENTUALLY, WITH ALL this material read and digested, Vatsya started writing. There is no record of how long he took, but the result was certainly short, snappy and readable: a book of seven fat chapters, each of which carried between two and 10 sub-sections, and the sum total of which would take no longer than a day to read.

Before we go any further, we must take pains to disassociate the work we are describing from the widely known version of the *Kama Sutra* popularized in the West. That volume is merely a catalogue of sexual positions. There are numerous references to the *Kama Sutra* in Western culture, in books, movies and on websites, and in almost all references the list of ways in which a man and a woman can copulate is presented as if it is the original work in its entirety. In fact, this list of positions is part of the *Kama Sutra*, but only a small part of it. It is a sub-division of one chapter. The rest of the book is a wide-ranging discussion of the philosophies of human interaction, and touches upon a great many other subjects. Furthermore, the prurient tone that is associated with reading the *Kama Sutra* in modern times is off-target. The book is not a work of erotica in any way. It is a factual compilation of facts written by a man for whom ethical and religious issues were fundamental issues. This is not to say that it does not make for eye-opening, somewhat arousing reading. Ironically, the list of positions for copulation makes rather bland, anti-erotic reading. But in the other chapters, the parts that are inevitably removed, there are genuinely erotic discussions of the pleasures of kissing, biting, scratching, "accidental" touching and the subtle arts of seduction.

Once Vatsya started writing, he himself was probably surprised at how wide-ranging his work became. For example, the book also discusses issues that anticipate Calvinism, such as the predestination of individuals to wealth or poverty. "People who believe that the prime mover of all things is destiny, say: 'Why should one work to get rich? You can work hard, yet fail. Or you can do no work at all, and get a windfall. Destiny is the lord of gain and loss, success and defeat, pleasure and pain.'" This sort of thinking was defeatist and should be avoided, Vatsya argued. "You have to exert yourself to get anything in life; that's a basic principle. If you want a great deal, you have to exert yourself a great deal, and that remains true even if you are destined for success."

Vatsya was criticized by people focused on wealth creation—the *artha* scholars—for spending so much time working on a guide to pleasure. They complained that focusing on pleasure would lead scholars into "contact with low people," and lives of sin. Furthermore, people who devoted their lives to pleasure lost the respect of others, and usually ended up in a bad way.

The scholar agreed that these dangers were accurately associated with taking an interest in physical pleasures, but argued that their existence was no reason to completely forgo such pleasures. "You don't forgo cooking your dinner, just because you may attract a beggar who asks you for some of it. You don't forgo planting seeds, just because the deer may eat them," he retaliated. The right thing to do was to balance your life. You need different elements particularly the big three: *dharma*, *artha* and *kama*, or virtue, material possessions and pleasure.

But as he got further into it, the book continued to veer off course. In some parts, he was not just summarizing previous thoughts but making a series of controversial statements—including arguing that women should read it; and not just married women, but unmarried maidens, too. This raised the ire of men, who felt that such knowledge was only suitable for their sex. Vatsya scoffed at this narrow-minded stance. After all, men needed women for traditional sexual relationships. He felt that women naturally knew a great many of the laws of relationships, even if they did not know them in the scientific manner that a man may known them. You cannot keep women from knowing about the lore of sensual relationships, because "women already know the *Kama Sutra*," he argued. You can become an expert in something simply by doing it, without ever learning the scientific terms for what you are doing, he wrote.

Mind you, he was a decorous, well-bred man, and balked at the improper idea of older men teaching it to girls or women—and he wanted married women to at least ask their husbands before they read it. He suggested that women should study it in groups by themselves, or in the presence of a close female confidante.

The work ranges widely, starting with sections carrying titles such as "The Conduct of the Well-Bred Townsman." This section offers an outline of the perfect day in the life of a refined man, and gives a great deal of general advice: "Shave the head every four days," but "wash the armpits every day." There is a section on "Acquiring a Wife," warning readers that they should make sure the girl is relaxed after they are introduced to her. Don't strut around and show off. Make sure she doesn't feel threatened. There are sections on touching, such as "Petting and Caresses" and "The Art of Scratching." He also included practical advice, such as "The Task of Go-Betweens" and "How to Look for a Steady Lover." Much of the work is concerned with good behavior, and there are copious lists of women who should not be approached for sex (such as your neighbor's wife, or the wife of the king). Then there is the infamous section on sexual positions. While some of these are quite creative, there is a curiously mathematical element about it. He argued that there are eight basic positions and eight basic movements, so that makes up 64 possible actions.

Although the scholar intended to spend his time summarizing the works of others, he soon found himself editing, adding and censoring. There were many things he disagreed with. At some stage in his work, he found he could no longer keep his opinions to himself, and he started commenting on the data he was transcribing. Indeed, there are several passages where he found himself quoting the works of the Babhuravya school, and then telling the reader why the experts were wrong. "The disciples of Babhuravya say…" he would begin. And then, referring to himself in the third person, he would add: "But Vatsyayana says…"

Above all, Vatsya recommended getting a good education—and unusually for that day and age, he thought this was particularly true for women. He made long lists of Things That People Should Know. He thought of them as "the arts." These not only included classical areas of female-friendly knowledge such as music, cooking, sewing and perfume making, but also sorcery, tongue-twisters, accessorizing, playing tunes by tapping glasses of water and "making parrots out of yarn." Becoming highly educated was a sort of insurance policy against misfortune, he argued. "If a wife becomes separated from her husband, and finds herself in a bad situation, she can support herself easily, even in a foreign country, by means of her knowledge of these arts," he said. "Even a basic knowledge of them makes a woman attractive, though putting them into practice depends on the circumstances of each case."

He also recommended that men educate themselves in all the arts possible, because it was one of the best tools they could have for charming women: "A man who is versed in these arts, and who is chatty and familiar with gallant behavior, quickly wins the hearts of women, even though he hasn't known them for very long."

He highlighted the importance of education by pointing to the existence in India at that time of the *pithamardas*: men who had no wealth other than their education. We can think of these individuals as "barefoot professors" who would attach themselves to wealthy patrons. "A *pithamarda* is a man without wealth, alone in the world, whose only property consists of his stick, his soap and his towel, who comes from a good country, and who is skilled in all the arts; and by teaching these arts is received in the company of citizens, and in the abode of public women." Women in those days were divided into two basic categories: private and public. The private ones were the ones you married, and to whom middle and upper caste families gave birth. Public ones were courtesans, but were not despised as prostitutes in the modern way. They were attractive, independent-minded women who exchanged any chance of living traditional "kept" wife-and-mother roles for the freedom to live independently.

They tended to work as professional temporary partners to the wealthy. This sort of woman was fully entitled to use her wiles to get men to fall in love with her, and then to take all their money; indeed, this was their duty, Vatsya said. "The duty of a courtesan is to form relationships with suitable men after due consideration, and make them feel strongly attached to her. And then to get all the man's money and possessions before dismissing him." The underlying meaning of this argument is rather modern, especially if we put it into today's colloquial speech. He is saying to female readers who chose the role of independent women: "He thinks he is screwing you, but you should screw him."

But everyone—courtesans included—are expected to live by the highest principles of *dharma*. He proposes that courtesans who make a lot of money devote some of it to building temples and parks and other purposes that are ultimately to the worship of God.

Vatsya was a details person. Not for him were those general books of advice that enjoined men to be strong and manly. No, he went into enormous detail about how to woo a woman. Arrange to meet the woman you love at social occasions, and then send out signals that wordlessly show your interest, he recommended. "The man should be careful to look at her in such a way as to cause the state of his mind to be made known to her; he should pull at his moustache, make a sound with his nails, cause his jewelry to tinkle, bite his lower lip, and make various other signs of that description," he said.

Wit was the secret of winning a woman's heart. "A conversation having two meanings should be carried on," the scholar recommended. Subtle signals and good humor: that was the way to win the heart of the person you fancy, the *Kama Sutra* says. And don't forget to tug at your moustache and tinkle your jewellery.

Several of the books he was summarizing discussed the way that powerful people could acquire relationships for themselves. Power was an aphrodisiac in itself, and people in power could control situations and employ go-betweens to make relationships blossom in ways that they may not do so naturally. Kings often felt they were entitled to have relationships with anyone they liked, and in some of the fiefdoms that made up India, rulers could demand sexual access to any women—wives, daughters or even the newly wed. But the scholar reckoned that this was a bad idea. From his point of view, it was asking for trouble. He dug up examples of rulers who had entered the homes of others to dally with their wives and been caught. "Abhira, the king of the Kottas, was killed by a laundryman while in someone else's house, and in the same way, Jayasana, king of the Kashis, was slain by the commander of his cavalry."

In the more sophisticated cities, the principles laid down by the great leaders of the past, mostly during the rule of the Maurya family, actually limited the power of the rulers. Neither kings nor their chief ministers were legally allowed to march into the properties of landowners. Nor could they demand access to their subject's wives and daughters. If a powerful man was attracted to the wife of another, he would have to seduce her. Vatsya suggested using a go-between to make the king's wishes known to the woman in question, and assure her of (a) generous gifts if she agreed and (b) secrecy so that no one would know. If the woman refuses the offer, she should still be given a gift, and the go-between should part with her on good terms. In other words, women were entitled to say *No*.

But after listing various ways in which rich and powerful men could win the hearts of other men's wives, Vatsya concluded that none of these were really a good idea, for the ruling classes had an important task of setting an example. "Their mode of living is constantly watched and observed and imitated by the general public. Animals see the sun rise and they get up; they see the sun lay himself down in the evening, and they do the same. People are no different. Persons in authority should therefore not do anything in public which is improper, deserving of censure, or beyond the range of acts allowed by virtue of their position."

Vatsya ends the section on seducing other men's wives by turning full circle, and pointed out that good leaders would not want to do any of these things. It's almost as if he is saying: *Why are you reading this chapter anyway?* "The above and other ways are the means used in various places by leaders who wish to interact with other men's wives. But a leader who has the welfare of his people at heart should not on any account put them into practice," he wrote. "A ruler who has conquered the six enemies of mankind, becomes the master of the whole earth." In India, there were six "deadly sins," and these were: Lust, Anger, Avarice, Spiritual Ignorance, Pride and Envy.

Perhaps because of his religious background, Vatsya was a moralistic man and did not hold sway with the sort of underhanded trickery that Chanakya would have applauded. The scholar was outraged to read that the followers of Babhravya recommended paying a young woman who was good at gossiping to associate with one's wife and find out her secrets, such as exactly how chaste she was. Vatsya declared that entrapments such as this were morally wrong: how can you drag someone down and then condemn them for falling? "A man should not cause his innocent wife to be corrupted by bringing her into the company of a deceitful woman," he said.

All in all, there was a great element of mystery in relationships. Women had great subtlety, he wrote, and "natural intelligence." You can't fully understand them. "Women are hardly ever known in their true light, though they may love men, or become indifferent toward them, or may give them delight, or may abandon them, or may extract from them all the wealth they have."

Taken as a whole, it is not a book of erotica, but a fascinating window into the politics of interpersonal relationships in Indian society in the fourth century CE.

At the end of the book, Vatsya included a stern warning: "This work is not to be used merely as an instrument for satisfying our desires." He explained that the other key parts of a person's life (that is, virtue and material possessions, or *dharma* and *artha*), were more important than pleasure, *kama*. If a man balanced these three factors, "without becoming the slave of his passions, he will obtain success in everything he does." It is not the sex manual that most people think it is, but a wise, brave, eye-opening and amusing book.

## THE ELEMENTS OF YOUR LIFE

THE ACTIONS YOU TAKE are reflected three ways, said Vatsya. They may be *dharma*—positive duties that increase the amount of virtue in the world. They may be *artha*—they may increase your material possessions. Or they may be *kama*—things you do purely for pleasure's sake.

Vatsyayana was worried that people did not balance the three elements, but tended to favor one at the expense of the others. This, in his view, was always wrong. Certainly, it is as easy to find examples of ill-balanced activity today as it was in his day.

Too much *dharma*: I recall having a long meeting with a charity worker whose project was a wonderfully inspiring task that sent help to where it was much needed in South Asia. But the directors of the charity were woefully out of touch with economics and principles of governance (*artha* in the sense that the sage

Chanakya would have used the word). Indeed, one of the items on the charity worker's list was to raise enough funds to pay for her own salary. This was clearly a project with a millstone around its neck. To raise money for the needy and to raise money for herself were two very different aims, with different motivations and needing very different sales techniques. Worse still, there was definite potential for her actions to be seen as involving impropriety. The way the organization had been organized, she was promoting the needy, but some of the money she raised needed to go into her own pocket. Although I offered what help I could on a project-by-project basis, I did not tie myself too deeply with this charity, merely urging them to learn more about how charities needed to be structured. This was definitely a case that had lots of *dharma*, in the sense of goodwill, and not enough *artha*, in the sense of economic sense.

Too much *kama*: This, sadly, is widespread. The pleasure principle is everywhere. We are exhorted to do things not because they are right, but because they are fun. And then we end up believing that we shouldn't have to do anything which isn't fun. At my children's school the parents were asked to raise funds to buy computerized interactive whiteboards for the classrooms. This was because teachers said: "It increases the *wow* factor of our lessons." At the same time, educationists published reports saying that they were seriously concerned about the high rate of hyperactivity and low level of concentration of modern children. The youngsters had lost the ability to sit down and get lost in a book. It became obvious to some parents that the problem was too much "wow factor" and not a shortage of it. These days, young people are surprised and aggrieved when they have to do anything that is not motivated entirely by pleasure. Today, they say "I'm bored" if the barrage of digital entertainment stops for a few minutes. So what do we do? We buy them portable DVD players and iPods so that they can never, never be alone with their thoughts. We don't realize that those precious times that children are alone with their thoughts are among the most important times of all: that's when they are growing, that's when they are working things out, that's when they are forming their personalities, that's when they are gaining emotional intelligence and growing that elusive but all-important thing called character. When a child says "I'm bored," smile. Give him or her a cushion, a glass of milk and a window to stare out of or an interesting task to do or a picture book to read. Feed his *dharma* instead of his *kama* for a while.

Too much *artha*: This is so endemic that I barely need to look for examples. They are all around us, all the time. I would say the majority of corporations today sacrifice their ethics to their desire for profit. The code phrase for this is "looking after the shareholders' interests." Wherever you see this phrase or the same concept in different words, you'll find that someone is making excuses for doing something bad in the name of profit. This phrase is a red flag. Run a mile from anyone who uses it. It is thinly disguised code for an admission of evil. They have sacked a large number of staff after having promised to do no further downsizing; they have dropped their *pro bono* projects; they have canceled their sponsorships after promising money to education or the arts or sports; they have found a clash between doing the right thing and increasing profits, and they have chosen to increase profits. Sometimes they realize that we know what they are really saying, so they guiltily defend themselves by saying: "We are legally obliged to look after our shareholders' interests." This is merely a way of sidestepping the issue by implying that all shareholders automatically demand that companies chose profit over ethics, which is clearly untrue. So great is the worship of the bottom line today that feeding it takes precedence over all other factors. These business people are damaging *dharma* in the name of *artha*.

Despite presenting these three factors as a triumvirate of leading lights, Vatsya went out of his way to put them in order of precedence. *Dharma* takes first place and must not be moved from that position, said the apostle of *kama*. Doing your duty and making sure that what's right comes first, and is above all things. *Artha* comes second: if you don't look after your material needs, you disadvantage yourself. Only if you have food and shelter, can you turn your mind to other things. And *kama* went third in the list of priorities. If you have to sacrifice something, you should sacrifice the time set aside for pleasure. Although he described *kama* as being "as necessary for well-being as food," it was important for him that people knew they should put first things first.

In today's society, we have things badly mixed up. *Artha* and *kama* are elevated above all things. Television shows bombard us with wide-angled views of how the super-rich live, and tell us in excruciating detail how to dress like them, decorate our homes to look like theirs and prepare meals like their chefs do. Wealth and pleasure are everything. Magazines and newspapers are filled with details of the decadent, high-spending lives of celebrities. A few years ago, newspapers had a tiny space labeled "Thought for the day"—a centimeter or so every day for a bit of *dharma*. These have almost entirely disappeared. Even a centimeter is considered too much.

Today, factories around the world are devoted to building cars designed only to operate at their best above the legal speed limits. Why? Because people want them: they are flashy and cool and expensive and who cares about the rules, anyway? Rules are there mainly to protect the poor and the stupid and who gives a toss? The profit principle and the pleasure principle rule our planet. Virtue and duty are seen as archaic terms, only fit for religious cranks or the hopelessly old-fashioned. Ethics are for greenies or lefties or the wooly-minded. And Vatsya's pleas for balanced lives? They have all been edited out of the versions of his work that are most widely circulated.



## LESSONS FROM THE LIFE OF A CELIBATE SEX-EXPERT

LIKE CHANAKYA, THE WORLD'S first management guru, and Ashoka, the emperor of peace, Vatsyayana gives us two different routes to share his wisdom. His life and work in itself provides inspiration, and his writings are an additional source of valuable teaching. But one principle cannot be missed in this young man's life, and it is this:

***A single good decision can make history and transform your life.***

This is one of the scariest, and at the same time, most energizing principles that guides the ambitious person. It is hard enough to make a good decision; but once you think about all the repercussions it may have, one can be overpowered by the range of possibilities. Will I be wildly successful if I join this company or that one? Will I make it big if I become part of a big corporation or strike out on my own? To be a winner, should I focus on providing this service or that service? Will this book idea of mine be a worldwide bestseller, or that one?

These questions are all relevant, they are all significant, and they should all be ignored. Any question that can only be answered by an ability to read the future is not useful. Indeed, it is a negative influence, which serves only to distract you. Here we go back to the principle of living in the present, not the future, and certainly not the past. Like Arjuna, you have to focus all your energies on the present moment and the present issues.

Make sure you get those factors correct: they will take up all your energy, and they are the only things that count. If you take care of the present, the now, the moment in which you live, the future will take care of itself.

This does not mean that you should not plan for the future; not at all. Indeed, one of the key factors in deciding your present actions should be your future goals. So the long-term plan comes *before* the short-term decisions, not after them. Too many people drift through life with no thought of how they will live in the future. One of the great lessons of the *Bhagavad Gita* is to expect the inevitable. This sounds so obvious, yet few of us do it. We know it is inevitable that we will become old, yet many of us fail to arrange pension funds for ourselves. We know it is inevitable that competitors will move into our niche; yet few of us put time and energy into the innovation and market-expansion that will enable us to keep our customer base growing. We know it is inevitable that today's exciting new product will one day be yesterday's boring old product; yet few of us put the necessary energy into re-inventing our products, services or ourselves, to keep everything fresh and new.

All these crises can be avoided simply by accepting that the inevitable will happen; by putting some thought into being ready for the future; by facing reality. This applies to all manufacturers, whether you are making canned pumpkin soup or writing pop tunes. Don't worry about whether this song you have composed or that one will make you famous. That's not your job. Your audience will decide that. Your job is to be aware of your career as a whole; think about how you can use your musical skills to build up a career with a variety of strings to your bow (playing live, recording or teaching), and how you can build a healthy retirement fund.

Once you have decided this, then you break up that career into little chunks: what you need to do this decade; what you need to do this year, what you need to do this month, this week, today. And you will find that today's task is to compose a piece of music as a signature tune for a television show. Maybe the tune makes you famous. Then again, it may not. That's not an issue over which you have control. The issue you do have control over is whether it is good work or not. So make sure it's great work—your finest piece yet. Focusing all your energy on the deed, not its repercussions, will help you reach your goal for the day. And reaching your goal for this 24-hour period is the necessary step you need to take every day to reach your ultimate goals in life.

Vatsya did not intend to make his name reverberate through history. But he knew that if he published a major piece of freshly researched work, it would shape his career at the university. It would possibly get him a title as a professor. He set himself a clear, but rather challenging task. He had to collect documents that, allegedly, ran in a straight line from the very beginning of time itself.

He had no database or Internet connection. He had his university library and the works at whatever other institutions he could connect with. If he had to travel to another university to get a book, it would means days or weeks of travel. And yet he wrote his book—and it became a classic that has stood the test of time.

How best to plan for the future while focusing on the present? The simple adage that sums it up best is surely this one: *Plan your life as if you will live forever; live each day as if it were your last.*

***Find the opportunity under your nose.***

Most innovators discover a new principle or invent a new product. We admire them, because we know how hard it is to do this, and how difficult it is to succeed in today's jam-packed marketplace. Even the most prolific inventors produce more misses than hits.

And even if the idea is sparklingly original, sometimes it doesn't work: there are a million unpredictable factors that decide whether a product is a hit or not.

Vatsya had a huge hit: but he invented nothing. The idea of writing a book summarizing what was known about sensual pleasure was not original. Many people had done it before. The material in the book is not original. Although he added personal comments, the facts in the book are from other works. Even the title of the book, which was first known as *Vatsyayana's Kamasutra*, is not original: it is merely a label derived from the umbrella word for erotic lore, *kamashastra*.

So what was the magic that made him famous? Vatsya can be seen as one of the world's first marketing geniuses. He repackaged what he knew about human motivations and realized that people would be interested in reading a certain type of material. And he saw that this particular material was, in theory, freely available. But there were transmission problems between producer and supplier: there was too much material, it was unfocused, it was widely scattered and it was difficult to access.

So he became the facilitator. He read all there was to read, and then he boiled it down into chunks that could be easily assimilated. He put it out as a relatively small volume, and it became more popular than all the other editions put together. Indeed, it became the only edition that has stayed in print for centuries.

The principle that Vatsya used is one that we know well today: we call it "adding value." It's an alternative form of business development to the standard technique where you create a new product or a new service. Instead, you take something that already exists and you alter it in some way to add value to it. It's a way of working that has far less risk than creating and marketing new things. The person who adds value is working with a supply and demand situation that already exists. There is already movement there. All he is doing is making adjustments that increase the flow, and profiting from his level of success in achieving that.

***Tap into your customers' deepest motivators.***

We do things because we are motivated to do them. The word "motivate" comes from the same root as the word "motor," indicating something that powers movement. Psychologists have long known that the deepest human motivator is the desire to stay alive; first, by keeping our own bodies alive, and second, by giving birth to progeny, and thus keeping our genetic line living forever. In other words, we are driven at the deepest level by the desire to avoid death and have the relationships that will produce offspring.

In practical terms, the desire to stay alive is manifest in our need for food and shelter. If you drop a human being into a landscape with no equipment or friends, the first thing he or she will do is find sources of food and water, and build a shelter to keep the elements at bay. These are primal needs. And once they are served, the human will quickly move to find a close friend or mate. A partner is also a very basic need.

After that, we move to a third layer. The person needs to find his or her place in society. He or she needs to become part of the social system, join the great mechanism that enables us to function as team players, take our place as a partner in the grand human enterprise. We need to be plugged in to our communities. This level splinters into a hundred different options. You suddenly have a great many choices and decisions to make. What opportunities are there? Where can I get a job? Where can I fit in?

And once that level is sorted out, we get to the final level, the topmost level: we need to find personal fulfillment. Here the number of options explodes, and the choices and decisions run into the tens of thousands. How do we fulfill ourselves? Can I find a job that really satisfies me? What should my hobbies be? Should I join some sort of club or church or temple? *How should a man live?* Finding fulfillment is not easy. There are psychological needs that we barely know we have. Psychologists say that most of us have "unwritten promises to our parents."

We had experiences when we were young that shaped our lives, often without our being aware of them. We have phobias that need to be conquered and aspirations that need to be met. Our individual personalities come to play here. To one person, the most important thing is that he is celebrated; to the next person, the vital thing is to conform; to the third, the crucial thing is to be respected; to the fourth, the essential thing is to create art that is appreciated.

Where does "making money" fit into all of this? It may not be clear at first glance. Money is a relatively recent invention, only some 3,000 years old. (In India, cows were used as currency for centuries before coinage was developed.) But money enables us to move through all the layers of need, smoothly and easily. It is the *uber*-layer, running from the bottom to the top of the needs pyramid. It helps us find food and shelter, and that in turn gives us space and time to woo a partner; money gives us options in choosing where we fit into society, and it finances our wildest flights of fantasy as we try to find personal fulfillment.

When we produce a product, we often focus on our need to create: we feel an urge to market that widget, start that factory, write that book, open that restaurant, produce that movie and so on. We are operating from our own level four and level five motivators. We are looking to establish our place in society and we are looking for personal fulfillment. This is all well and good. But we also need to look at our customers' needs. What motivates them? We are only going to be successful if we fulfill their needs.

If your product or service only fulfils a level five need, it's going to be a niche product. But if it serves a level one need, it will appeal to everyone.

Let's look at practical examples. Every few years, a volume is produced with a title such as *The Wedding Cake Decorator's Handbook*. This is clearly a niche product, appealing to a small subgroup of level five. But books by authors such as Stephen Covey and Deepak Chopra appeal to our level one and level two needs: they help us sort out our lives from the bottom upward, helping us to sort out our financial security and our interpersonal relationships. They help us with our more basic needs. Niche books are often produced in print runs of just 400 to 1,000 copies. Mass market paperbacks about money and relationships are often produced in tens of thousands of copies.

Be aware of the deepest motivations of your customers. It will help you design marketing material that will touch them. And it will increase sales exponentially. An example: For much of the 20$^{th}$ century, the condom was a niche product. It was just one option among many for sexually active people who wanted to avoid pregnancy. And condoms were often seen as the least attractive or comfortable of the contraceptive options around. Yet the rise of HIV/AIDS in the 1980s saw the product completely repositioned. Condoms suddenly became the simplest practical way of protecting yourself from a killer disease. The advertising and marketing changed. It went from a level five option to a level one necessity. Sales quickly doubled and continue to escalate.

## THE MAGIC REDISCOVERED

VATSYA'S BOOK WAS A big hit in India. It would have to have been a success to have stayed in print for so long during an era when books were copied by hand. Of course, literacy was not widespread, so it was not carried around by members of the general public like a modern day popular thriller. But it became widely known among the educated classes. Every library had a copy, and the wealthy would have had their personal editions, hand-copied for them. Yet while most "hit" books have their moment in the sun, Vatsya's book of love transcended them all, becoming the equivalent of a religious text, copied and re-copied, handed down from generation to generation, century after century. But it was purely an Indian text for India alone—until it became famous around the world after it was translated into English in 1883.

It happened thus. The legendary British explorer Sir Richard Burton was in India working with local scholars on translations of Indian classics. He was amused to hear that there were several classics on the theme of love and sex. Each volume tended to encapsulate and summarize the ones before them: that was the Indian way. So he decided that he should read the latest one, which would thus include much of the lore of the earlier ones. This was *The Anunga Runga or Kamaledhiplava*. The title could be translated as "The Stage of Love or A Boat in the Ocean of Love." It was composed by a poet named Kullianmull, for the amusement of Ladkhan, a prince of the House of Lodi, which reigned in India from 1450 to 1526 CE. In the Indian scale of time, this book, being only three or four centuries old, was considered "the most recent bestseller" on the market.

Sir Richard discovered that it had been translated into English once before, but the print run was only six copies. All had gone into the libraries of the rich. The more he studied this genre, the more amazed he became. While other civilizations, his own included, dealt with the subject of love under a thick, romantic layer of poetry, here were scholars bluntly examining every aspect of it, ethical, spiritual and physical, in the plainest of language, with detailed descriptions. Men and women and their actions were classified in the same way that "writers on natural history have classified and divided the animal world," he told his colleagues.

He was fascinated to hear about the theory of the Lotus Woman—the perfect female. She had a beautiful face, a perky bosom, a soft, fleshy body (signified by three folds across her stomach), a voice "as low and musical as the song of the Kokila bird," and she was both spiritually aware and highly intelligent.

This was jolly good stuff and should be made available to the English-speaking world, he decided. (Sir Richard was taking the role of re-packager, just as Vatsya had.) The British Orientalist decided to get together a team of pundits to translate the *Anunga Runga*. But as they worked on the text, he was struck by the number of references to the mysterious Vatsya. The author of the book constantly related his work to the thoughts of the love-sage Vatsya, who was referred to with great respect.

"Who was this Vatsya fellow?" Sir Richard eventually asked.

"He is the author of the standard work on love in Sanskrit literature," one of the pundits replied. "No Sanskrit library is complete without his work."

Sir Richard expressed an interest in seeing this ancient book, but was told that it was very old indeed, and today most libraries had only sections or fragments of it. It might be difficult to get a trustworthy, complete copy. The explorer decided that it would be more worthwhile for all concerned if they abandoned the *Anunga Runga* and instead worked on the writings of the sage of love: first, putting together a trustworthy complete copy in Sanskrit, before doing an English translation.

They found a copy at a library in Bombay, but it seemed damaged and incomplete, so they requested manuscripts from university libraries in Varanasi, Calcutta and Jaipur. Then they found a detailed commentary called *Jayamangla,* which was several centuries old.

The pundits got to work. After months of toil, the chief pundit wrote a note to Sir Richard. "The accompanying manuscript is corrected by me after comparing four different copies of the work. I had the assistance of a commentary called *Jayamangla* for correcting the portion in the first five parts, but found great difficulty in correcting the remaining portion, because, with the exception of one copy thereof which was tolerably correct, all the other copies I had were far too incorrect. However, I took that portion as correct in which the majority of the copies agreed with each other."

Sir Richard found the resultant book to be a thoughtful and eye-opening window on to the most intimate parts of life in India one and a half millennia earlier. He pointed out that Christians said authors may rest in peace but their works live on after them. "Yes, indeed, the works of men of genius do follow them, and remain as a lasting treasure," he wrote in the commentary of the translated English edition he eventually published. "And though there may be disputes and discussions about the immortality of the body or the soul, nobody can deny the immortality of genius, which ever remains as a bright and guiding star to the struggling humanities of succeeding ages. This work, then, which has stood the test of centuries, has placed Vatsyayana among the immortals, and on This, and on Him no better elegy or eulogy can be written than the following lines:

*So long as lips shall kiss, and eyes shall see,*
*So long lives This, and This gives life to Thee."*

By appending this *faux*-Shakespeare quote to Vatsya's work, we can see how Sir Richard viewed the book. Not as pornography, but as a classic distillation of human thought by a writer of genius.

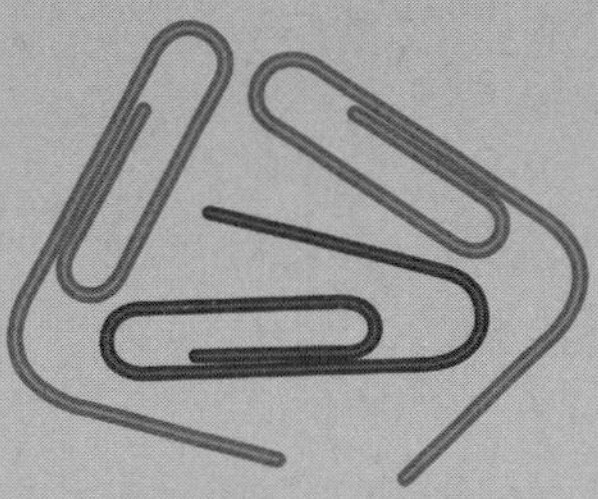

# FURTHER TRAVELS IN ANCIENT WRITINGS

# 9

**INNER JOURNEYS CAN TAKE YOU A LONG WAY. BUT THIS BOOK IS MERELY THE FIRST STEP ON A MUCH LONGER TRIP.**

## DOORS SHUT, OTHERS OPEN

WE'RE REACHING THE END of our journey. This was a joy to write; I hope the reader will get at least half the pleasure reading this work as I had in putting it together. But I also hope this is more than just a mildly interesting mix of business inspiration and under-appreciated ancient history; perhaps it will go a small way toward filling a gap.

Thousands of history textbooks and encyclopedias around the world focus on early civilizations, and always the same few are mentioned: the Mesopotamians, overseers of "the cradle of civilization;" the ancient Egyptians, with their magnificent monuments that define the category of "wonders of the ancient world;" and China, which continually reminds us that it is a civilization with 5,000 years of history.

India is rarely mentioned in these contexts. Yet archeological discoveries have been made, and are still being made, that indicate the subcontinent was the place where the human race made many of its key discoveries. Thanks to the Meluhhans, historians now know that the Indian region was the location of the first planned cities, the first wheeled transport, the first spun cotton, the oldest writing and so on. Those ancient days were of great historical import: the activities on the Indus River plain shaped modern urban society. And it would have been at that place, alongside contemporary trading partners in Mesopotamia and Egypt, that it became evident that organized, concentrated humanity could produce marvelously complex and wealthy settlements, with regular surpluses that could be exchanged overseas. This led to the development of international trade and ultimately urban development—a boring phrase with an attractive meaning: it means human family settlements become happier, more secure places, and starvation and deprivation are banished. Many places on earth are still waiting to make that journey.

The Meluhhans made some remarkable discoveries about the generation of wealth—but the same part of the world produced Siddhartha Gautama, who made another great human discovery, which was that wealth and human fulfillment were not the same thing. The acquisition of material possessions actually did not lead to satisfaction and perfection. Siddhartha asked the great question: *How should a man live?* And he came up with an answer that has lost none of its value today. Twenty-four centuries ago, the Awakened ones began to take humanity on an inner journey, a trip that people still take today to seek personal fulfillment.

India also plays a key role in the dawn of literature. The Aryans were responsible for Vedic literature such as the *Rig Veda*, which is 3,500 years old, more ancient than any of the texts in the Bible or the Koran. Only very few pieces of literature are older: *The Epic of Gilgamesh* from Sumeria, which is about 4,000 years old, and a couple of pieces from Egypt that are 3,800 years old.

There are other Indian classics, too, which are ancient and venerable. From the fourth century BCE we have the *Mahabharata* and the *Ramayana*, two ancient national epics. In this book, we have not had space to review them in detail, but they are well-represented by the celebrated but hard-to-read *Bhagavad Gita*, which we have discussed at length.

And then we have the marvelous characters of Indian history. Among the great kings of India, Ashoka Piyadassi, Beloved of the Gods, created an amazing society that blended humanitarian and environmental ideals into a system of governance: a remarkable achievement that seemed to be millennia ahead of its time. His personal journey from warrior of blood to envoy of care is as inspiring as was his completion of his stone diary—a message to the future that was lost for centuries but has now been deciphered, to the world's immeasurable benefit.

And there was the curious religious scholar Vatsya, whose lively but misunderstood book has framed this voyage through ancient Indian legends. The author of *Kama Sutra* was a modernist and a realist. He knew that money and material possessions were important—but so was pleasure. Yet pleasure should only be taken after due time and attention have been given to other things: first, to acts that directly benefit society, and second, to economic activity. His plea for balance in our lives has never been more relevant than it is today.

The personalities and stories mentioned above really deserve to each have a whole book to themselves. We haven't dug to any depth in this volume. We have provided only a sweeping overview, rather than a comprehensive examination. Perhaps we have done no more than to provide an introduction so that you may wish to get to know them better. Further reading will bring large dividends to the curious reader.

And as far as our coverage of Indian wisdom goes, there's a great deal that we haven't even approached. We have limited ourselves to a few ancient Indian texts from Hindu, Buddhist and Jain traditions, and we haven't touched on the magic of Muslim or Sikh India at all, or any of the great kings that came after Ashoka. We haven't looked at the body of literature known as the Vedas, or the Panchatantra stories, or the Jataka tales. We haven't considered Kalidasa, who is known as "the Sanskrit Shakespeare." Again, those topics each deserve separate volumes, and will richly repay any research the reader chooses to do.

And of course, this is the age of the Internet, which is a period of democratization of information. Readers are invited to contribute to this work, and to help it to evolve, by contacting the publisher and the author through www.wiley.com or through the author's personal website at www.nuryvittachi.com.

## KEY MESSAGES FROM THIS BOOK

THIS BOOK HAS MANY lessons in it, and it is hard to boil them down to a few brief principles that one can take away. Yet there are some messages that stand out clearly.

- *The longest journey is but a single step, repeated.*
- *To make a great achievement in human society, you need a great team.*
- *Learn from the past, but concentrate on the now.*
- *Products and services are not the source of wealth: human activity is.*
- *Above all things, we must fulfill our* dharma*: our duty to increase what is good and right and loving in this world.*
- *Plan for the future, but live for the day.*
- *Turn your primary focus away from material possessions and pleasure, and all good things will come to you—including material possessions and pleasure.*
- *Our outer journeys are short strolls compared to our inner journeys.*
- *Balance is everything.*

But human nature being what it is, I suspect it will not be the written principles that stick in our minds, but the people who wrote them and who lived them. So I am going to give the last word to the unforgettable Chanakya, the wily, sneaky, angry sage who went from being a professor of political science to a military strategist. After all, not only was he the author of the world's first management handbook, but he provided proof that it worked, by using it to build a huge empire.

I mentioned earlier that Chanakya had some similarities with Wile E. Coyote from the *Roadrunner* cartoon series, with his wildly imaginative schemes to defeat his enemy. I wasn't being totally facetious, as this extract from the *Arthashastra* shows:

> *You may find an opportunity to kill your enemy while he is at a holy place he goes to for purposes of worship or pilgrimage.*
>
> 1. *You can loosen the fastenings of a stone or a wall so that they drop on his head.*
> 2. *You can shower him with rocks from a high part of the building.*
> 3. *You can cause a metal rod in the ceiling to fall on him.*
> 4. *You can hide sharp objects inside the body of the idol and launch them at his head.*
> 5. *You can sprinkle poisonous powder on the area where he walks or sits.*
> 6. *You can give him a bunch of flowers which emit lethal gas.*
> 7. *You can doctor his chair so it falls apart, tipping him into a pit which you have lined with pointed spears.*

He goes on to recommend other techniques for dealing with difficult people. Why not tunnel into their homes and throw poisonous snakes at them? To get into the heart of your enemy's territory, dress in drag and get someone to carry a coffin in front of you: no one will interrupt a widow at a funeral. And a good way of escaping, he said, is to pretend to be a corpse and have your colleagues carry you away in a shroud. I did not include these bits of strategy in the "lessons we can learn from Chanakya" section. Today's business registrars would not be amused (unless you live in a totally lawless place, such as downtown Los Angeles on a Friday night, or Bihar or Shenzhen pretty much any day of the week).

But the appealing thing about this sage is that he, like India, is full of contradictions. Wildly pragmatic when it came to dealing with enemies, he was the soul of kindness when it came to looking after fragile people such as orphans, battered women, domestic helpers and so on. "The leader shall give money to orphans, old folk, the infirm, the afflicted and the destitute. He shall also give subsistence to destitute pregnant women and to the children to whom they give birth," he wrote. Here are some of the laws Chanakya wrote on how to treat slaves:

> *You will lose a sum equivalent to what you paid for your slave if you:*
> *Make him or her carry a corpse, sweep away sewage or handle food scraps;*
> *Make a female slave attend on a master while he is bathing naked;*
> *Hurt or abuse him or her; or*
> *Violate the chastity of a female slave.*
> *Indeed, if you violate the chastity of any nanny, cook or domestic servant, you immediately earn their freedom for them.*

Ultimately, he knew that the right relationship between the people and the government was the key to a happy society. "Taxation should not be painful for the people," he wrote. "Governments should collect taxes like a honeybee that sucks just the right amount of nectar from the flower so that both can survive." You can see the governments of low-tax jurisdictions such as Hong Kong and Monaco applauding that line.

This mixture of the hard and the soft, the aggressive and the peace-loving, the ambitious and the contented, is still with us today. A visit to India is an assault on the senses. It is a noisy, brash, garish, smelly destination. Yet simultaneously it is a place of great tranquility and spiritual wisdom. One can't attempt to understand it. One just has to take it all in and let it change one.

Ancient texts from India have clear value, and it is hoped that this exercise in resurrecting them will light a little flame for the glories of the past. And, with a bit of luck, this age-old wisdom will start to seep into the modern world.

Or, as Chanakya wrote:

*Oil poured on water,*
*a secret communicated to an unworthy person,*
*a gift given to a worthy recipient,*
*a sermon delivered to an intelligent listener:*
*these things, by virtue of their nature,*
*spread.*

# INDEX

L



M



N